D0983210

The Restored Soul

By

Sheryl Hatwood

Contents

Copyright

enable them to rectify any reference or credit line in subsequent editions.

This publication contains the opinions and ideas of its author(s) and is designed to provide useful advice regarding the subject matter covered.

Dedication

Dedicated to survivors of abuse who found their voice and decided to walk in the freedom of their truth!

Acknowledgment

To my husband, Darrick, who watched me struggle with my emotions, navigated me through the turbulent times by being there for me, holding and encouraging me to continue writing my story. I love you!

To my daughter, for providing your support and understanding how important it was for me to share my experiences. Your life is my strength to continue to do better. You are one my life's greatest gifts.

A special thanks to my parents, who never stopped loving me and kept pushing me to live courageously regardless of the odds. Thank you for no reason and thank you for every reason. Your influence in my life has been invaluable.

Also, to my siblings, extended family, and friends who nursed me, cried with me, and lifted me through my pains without judging me. Thank you for your support.

To my younger self, thank you for the lessons!

I acknowledge and value all the love that
surrounds me today!

Preface

This book is the authentic depiction of my personal experiences and encompasses accurate details relevant to my tragedies. The abuse I suffered became a cycle that self-perpetuated because I suppressed my pain. As long as I remained silent, I remained a victim and believed all my negative self-talk.

When I decided to write about my life, it was not originally to reveal. Only when I started writing, my soul began to purge the secrets. I was conflicted about whether to do a gloss over or boldly move forward and completely expose my past. The latter was decided after conversations and support from my husband, and I wrote my life as a theatrical play. The Wounded Soul was written solely to share my experience and not for entertainment. It did more for me than I could realize. My story has helped others and, conversely, has helped me accept my scars and not live behind the mask of how I wanted others to see me. I am open, transparent, and completely vulnerable. I've connected deeper into my faith, and I now see myself differently.

This is how I restored my soul and changed my story's title to speak from a position of healing. The title *The Restored Soul* reflects the transition from the wound to restoration. I have unsilenced my experiences and exposed my pain through my writings, which has given less power to the shame and embarrassment I once felt.

I do it all unapologetically!

I hope that by sharing my experiences, no one will live beneath the truth of who they are, and not allow the residue of their past to continue to shape them. The truth is the beginning of healing. I have allowed my life to speak; my greatest pains are now being used for a greater purpose.

The names and identifying details have been changed to protect the privacy of individuals.

Chapter 1 – Girl of Color

"Isn't it magical the way light works? It falls on objects, brightens them up, and composes a color out of them," the soul stated.

"I don't find it magical. If anything, light is biased or in the least a source of creating bias," I corrected. "I don't know if it adds colors or reveals them, but it never depicts the true colors, if they even exist."

A long silence ensued between us as the soul tried to decipher what I meant. A minute later, it came up with a counter-argument. *"I don't agree,"* it said. *"What we see in the daytime is merely a mirage constructed by our light receptors to absorb some colors, reflect some and make us swoon over the beauty of what, in fact, is just at the surface."*

12

"Hmm. Then probably there is no color in this world without the light," I contemplated. "Perhaps we aren't our true skin color – beige, sand, or black. Maybe this tree isn't its true color – green. Ever have a look at the tree at night?"

"Insightful! If it weren't for the sunlight reflecting the complexion, illuminating your identity and lived experiences, we could close our eyes and be viewed the same," the soul explained.

"Doesn't that make the nighttime more beautiful, almost neutralizing and bias-free? If only we could remember to keep the lights off," I pressed.

"It surely does. Daytime engages you in seeing the world around you but also exposes your imperfections while the nighttime allows

13

you to wander around the abandoned territories

of your mind. The territories which behold the

hidden treasures of thoughts which were

suppressed during the daytime while you were

busy judging the appearance of things." The

soul elaborated.

"See. Due to this and so much more, I

always wish for the night to fall so that we can

see the light in the dark. But then again, I'd

wonder if prejudice, discrimination, and racism

would still prevail in the night depending on

how dark a shade of grey a person is," I said

matter-of-factly.

The soul went silent, and I knew it had

nothing more to say.

My family and I were battling racism in an all-white community in Canada. My father, a man of principle and value, never let his color or culture define him in the manner his perpetrators did. If anything, he took pride in them. His self-assured demeanor and bold personality made the bigoted respond cautiously before crossing him. Being a man of vision and solid self-esteem, he instilled the same values in us; he saw things clearly in both the day and night. I solely saw the day! Despite being a forbearer of racial discrimination, in my naivety, I spent my life acclimating to a culture that did not represent me. The most vivid memory I recall was trying to fit in and not understanding that I should not have to navigate such challenges with no map. I never understood how to emerge victorious in

15

this struggle. Maybe the night was so much better.

Regardless of the odds, we were making do in a small, ground-level room of the Maple Lodge Hotel with gravel as our floor. Our abode was an almost furniture-less room stacked only with two beds, one for my parents and the other for my two other siblings and me. This was the only place that "allowed" us to stay until my dad strategized our alternative independence. It took four months! Our first home on a rental basis, but better than where we were before. My dad's motto – do not look at where you are as an indicator of where you will remain. Although I could not quite formulate life how my dad viewed it, I believed what he said. He was, in essence, our family's GPS. Unlike most navigation units, there were no U-turns, just decisive roads, albeit filled with racial discrimination. I faced racism. I didn't know what to call it back then; perhaps my parents had a few choice words for it.

In 1977, "Roots" premiered on TV. I did not understand its message, nor could I comprehend the implications. I was a target of my naivete in connecting the bullying I faced was related to "Roots" induced racism unless my father called it out.

One Saturday morning, while my mother was sitting quietly on a sofa and immersed in the Ebony magazine, my father returned from work. He entered the front door and took his place beside Mom. Routinely, he would greet her with a kiss and grab the newspaper, and ask, "what's for dinner" before sitting down in the living room with us. My brother and sister were elsewhere in the house. My parents engaged in casual conversations about the day. Busy doing my homework on the floor, I occasionally crawled up to the coffee table to grab myself a cookie.

"Hello, Daddy!" I crooned.

"Hello love, how are you doing?" Dad asked.

"Great! Got some homework to do."

"Wow. My daughter is becoming a responsible girl now," Dad smiled.

"Yeah."

"So," he flipped open the newspaper and asked, "how was school today?"

"School was okay. I have a quiz every day and not much time to play."

"I see. There will be enough time to play later in life. "You make sure you're prepared for the quizzes and keep getting good grades," Dad instructed.

"I will."

A long silence stretched until I came up with the question that was nagging me throughout the day.

"Daddy?"

"Yes, dear," he replied with his face still buried in the newspaper.

"I have a question for you," I said, innocently.

"Go ahead."

"What does 'nigger,' and 'kizzy' mean?" I asked, oblivious of the seriousness of the matter.

Both Mom and Dad lifted their heads from the newspaper and magazine in complete sync and sat upright on the couch.

"Why do you ask?" Dad replied in a concerned tone.

"Just *wanna* know. My classmates keep teasing me with names like that. They even laugh at me.

"What?" Dad reacted.

What does that mean?" I asked again.

Mom's face had a look of astonishment, and Dad's breathing became intentional. I returned to my workbook, awaiting to unravel the puzzle of my identity and respond to my

20

question, but nothing came. Mom and Dad looked at each other and struggled to get more information from me about the episodes in my class, trying not to let on its severity just yet.

"Did you report it to the principal?" My mother finally spoke.

"Yes, I did."

"And?" Dad asked.

"Nothing. Mr. Tate told me to avoid them and said that they are just kids, and I shouldn't listen to them."

"That's it?" Dad asked, irritation evident on his face and in his voice.

I still remember how casually I took it. Even when my parents were super concerned, I kept munching on the cookies and taking swigs of my milk. My parents were on their feet now, and I was on the floor, doodling a sketch of my family.

"Ridiculous!" Mom slammed. "Shame on Mr. Tate for letting go of such a sensitive issue. He, of all people, should know and teach the children to appreciate differences at his school better." She started pacing back and forth, the way she usually did when perturbed.

"Unbelievable!" Dad chimed. "He should've at least showed some concern, and at the least, filled us in on the incident."

I decided I should go to my room, leaving the concern I unknowingly created.

Unconcerned as always, my eyes would only open to the brutal realities when I could no longer avoid them, or when they were staring me right in the face.

"Not your fault since you were only eleven then and blind to the toxicity plaguing our culture," the soul alleviated my guilt.

"Wait!" Daddy stopped me, unsatisfied with the incomplete information I had provided him. "Did Mr. Tate contact the kid's parents?"

"I don't know, Daddy." I shrugged my shoulder and left the room with the plate of cookies in my hand.

"This is insane!" Mom complained. She grabbed the empty coffee cup from the table. "Nicole, she shouted, "no food in your room. Put the cookies on the kitchen table now!"

"Okay, Mother!"

Daddy paced back and forth alone in the room, shaking his head, muttering to himself. "I want the names of those kids. I'm going to school tomorrow."

My father was a man of custom and culture. His color was his pride and lifestyle, a doctrine set in stone, but he was appreciative of all cultures. Anyone who tampered with his values was questioned for theirs in return. My father was a master at conducting introspective conversations, given he was confident in who he was. Most people did not have the nerve to approach him with discriminatory remarks or beliefs since they knew they'd be given a reality check in no time. He was an overprotective father, and nothing short of a genius.

"How did it feel when you were labeled?" the soul inquired.

I was too young to make sense of the feeling. But all I learned at that moment was that the world wasn't colorless. At precisely that moment, I was awakened to the differences and learned how the world could abandon you if you don't fit their appearance and culture ideals.

"It's then you began to realize that you were different. The world is colorless; only the kids colored your vision and showed you their views of the world," the soul summarized.

Chapter 2 – The Power Within

The next sunrise was certain and on time every day. But it seemed to cheat me out of the darkness where it was easier to hide from the previous day's bullying. It would only be a couple of hours before I had to prepare for the slaughter of insults, which were also certain each day but at various times. Is this the world my parents have been preparing us for? Did my brother and sisters feel the same way?

"A good night's sleep can clean the slate of the previous day's offenses," the soul stated.

"Umm. Yeah, I guess. Healed to be reopened."

I wanted to sleep the day away but couldn't for two reasons; I was too young to exercise my own will, and secondly, because that does not happen in Jamaican families.

"You're fortunate that you have a bed to sleep in, parents who love you, and a home. Have you forgotten where you began?" the soul said, urging me to count my blessings.

I don't think we can compare one's suffering to another's because, in either case, you can't tell how much someone is hurting. In my case, not because I had it better than anyone, but because the message is a practiced mantra given to kids to be humbled into submission. Sleep was the only escape, the only source of healing I could find amid chaos.

The soul went silent and was not evoked until it could introduce me to a blessing that I had turned a blind eye towards.

I woke up at 8:00 a.m. the next day. My room was a neat mess as I had left it the night before. There were plaid green polyester pants, and a peach frilled top laid sloppily across my bed head. With those colors, I am sure my mom was preparing me to model in the vegetable section of the grocery store! My clothes had to be ready the night before and ironed if necessary. My hair was braided and wrapped in a headscarf to protect our hair's essential oils from being soaked up by the pillow. My childhood was structured and ran like an army camp. Once you get up, you had to say good morning to the whole household before venturing to start the day. If I forgot, it was considered a federal offense of disrespect.

28

I exchanged formalities with my parents, sisters, and brother and ventured on to start my day brushing my teeth, washing up, and getting dressed before going downstairs to eat breakfast. After breakfast, it was back to the bathroom to wipe the food stains off my mouth and return downstairs with the hairbrush, so Mom could brush up the curls that disobeyed the hair scarf. When everyone was ready, as a unit, she sent us out to the frontlines. And off to school we went.

School was associated with the same thing - the certainty of the name calling. Today, it was my brother who was attacked at recess. My brother was born when my mom had the German Measles. He was visually and hearing impaired. His clothing was decorated with the hearing aid device attached to the front jacket pocket and pop bottle glasses. He was an easy target for the kids; it became his routine. I could not understand the attacks. In fact, I thought we were special, not different! My little sister was the first black baby to be born in Plattsburgh, population 7,000. They chronicled her in the newspaper. She's like a notable person in Plattsburgh's history. We are special people not different – didn't the kids know that? I made it through another school day, protecting my brother from the new name they gave him – "Toby." We headed back to our safe zone, our home. How I wish my dad attended our school. No one would bother me then, I'm sure of it!

I made my way downstairs out of my bedroom into the living room. Unexpectedly in the living room, was my father sitting on the far end of the couch, with his left leg lurched forward. His concerned eyes followed me until I secured a place on the ground opposite the coffee table. Despite leaning back in the soft embrace of the sofa, his restlessness was apparent. One of his hands was stretched out around the couch while the other hand lightly tapped on his laps. I grabbed the workbook lying on the table and greeted him with a good afternoon. We were raised as royalty – formalities were important.

"Good afternoon, love," he said as he beamed at me genuinely.

A silence ensued until he called out my name, "Nikki."

"Yes, Daddy," I said.

"Here. Come," he gestured for me to sit next to him.

31

"Okay, Daddy." I obeyed and sat next to him, head down.

"Listen up. I was at your school earlier this afternoon and spoke with Mr. Tate about the incident you mentioned about the kids calling you names. He promised me that he'd speak with the parents of the kids who bullied you," he affirmed. I observed how my father held back his thoughts and carefully selected his words to impart the message. I simply nodded. "But him nevah even…," he trailed off in his Jamaican dialect before returning to his composed state. "I mean, he had this notion that kids are merely kids who tend to say and do what they watch on television. Which is to say, he wouldn't punish them," he continued and then paused.

The ramifications of the Roots series.

"So, do one thing for me," he said finally.

"Yes, Daddy?" Meanwhile, he got up and looked over the TV Guide as if searching for a specific program.

"Ah, okay. Let's watch this program," he turned on the TV to channel four. I silently watched what he was up to. Soon, I realized I was being made to watch a boxing match. He paused the program and said, "Watch!"

I glared at the TV and watched as one of the boxers battered his opponent badly, and the poor opponent couldn't let out anything apart from incoherent groans and mumbles.

"What am I looking at, Daddy?"

"Things that children watch on TV," my father retorted. Had I misapplied my view? I wasn't sure what I was looking at. I spared another glance at the boxing match, which displayed this one-sided fight so far. I gave my father a bewildered look, and he quickly got it.

"Okay. Go, turn off the TV," he plainly said. I did the same and secured my place next to him. "So, now I want you to imitate what you see on television."

"I don't get it, Daddy."

"Dear, I want you to defend yourself against any situation where you feel threatened," my father compelled.

"Huh?" I was too young to understand what this parable meant.

"Children imitate what they see on television, – according to Mr. Tate," he sarcastically said. "So, imitate what you saw on television a minute ago.

Here," he explained while motioning the space around his body. "This is your personal space. Never let anyone come near this space unless you know that they have good intentions."

I listened very intently to him because I could sense this was something serious; only I couldn't fully understand it yet.

"Hold on, one second," he got up and left the room. A few seconds later, he came with his boxing gloves. He put them on. Was he preparing me to be a champion fighter? After he fastened the oversized gloves on my hand, he stood in front of me and asked me to swing.

So, I did. The swing was not powerful.

"Come on, punch," he said intensely. "You can hit harder than that! Throw your body into it."

I swung. This time with a lot more power.

"That's right. Go on!" I started punching harder with all my force. "That's it. Perfect!"

I smiled confidently, knowing I just made my dad proud for some reason.

"So, what's the lesson of today?" my father questioned.

"To swing harder?" I said excitedly.

"No, dear. The lesson is to use Mr. Tate's reasoning why the children are calling you names to defend your reaction." He paused for a while to let the statement sink in. Then said, "Kids follow what they see on television, right?" he had a sly undertone, and I started to understand what he meant.

"So, what is good for one is good for another." He rhymed off in his Jamaican dialect. His Jamaican dialect always came out when he wanted to emphasize a point. I got it!

"Yes, Daddy," I cheerfully said and continued practicing my boxing swing until my father was satisfied. I remember getting too excited over my new learning as if I had mastered a new skill.

"Great. Now let's go and get something to eat, okay?" My dad seemed happy about the idea he equipped me with the skills to protect myself from a world that left me unprotected.

"Sure, Daddy."

On that note, I felt truly empowered in the flesh. I went to school and got suspended three times. Anyhow, I was cool with it since I had my father's permission to defend myself in any situation. My dad was more concerned that my behavior was being addressed but not those of the kids who taunted me. This was the world my father was preparing us for—a world with tainted sight and weighted wrongs based on the offender.

"How could you only empower a child physically without giving her insight into the inner self?" The soul returned.

My dad did the best he could to impart lessons he felt I had to learn, but I was not yet completely equipped to grasp the teachings. He had good intentions. I respect him for putting his family first, making us feel like we had a heavenly father here on earth.

Well, my classmates kept showering me with names, and I adopted an offensive rather than a defensive manner. Every name called was destined to meet my fist; that's just how I processed my hurt and grew into my new skill. My problem solving became easy. I learned to disguise my afflictions by an output of aggression.

Over the next three months, the name calling stopped. I established the boundaries. No one bothered my brother and me! Roots was a memory!

Another sunrise bloomed on the horizon, its golden petals stretching out and amalgamating into the richly blue hue. The brilliant yellow sky uncurled its warmth over the town, giving our lives an invitation to enter the new day. And so, we did. It was Saturday morning – chore time. Each of us knew what to do, and if we didn't, we were reminded only once! When we finished, we got snacks and could get our permissions to go for a bike ride, money for the candy store, or be free to roam around the house or in the backyard.

After our chores were completed, all my siblings sat around the coffee table, busy munching down snacks in the living room. Meanwhile, my mom was retrieving the clothes from the laundry basket and folding them perfectly. As usual, my dad was reading the newspaper and having quick swigs of peppermint tea at intervals. Almost out of the blue, he initiated a conversation with us.

"So, kids," he paused. "We have some good news for you."

I was thrilled as these two words 'good news' that escaped my father's mouth because I knew nothing ordinary would strike him as good news. I sat up and almost clapped. My siblings

and I were cheering and jumped excitedly on the
unheard news.

"Are we going on vacation, Daddy?" I
immediately guessed.

My siblings froze to hear the response.

"Um. No, and yes," my dad said, conjuring
up the right words to inform us about the news.

"Well," my mother intruded, "sort of. We
are moving to a new place."

"Wow!" I exclaimed. "Where? Please tell
me we are going to live near my friends and Mr.
Robinson. I'm his favorite girl. He can visit us
more every day, and I can get more candies or
go swimming." The simple rationalizations that
a child requires. Don't mess with my candy
supply. "Yeah," Mom said while folding
laundry clothes. "Cool your jets, baby girl. Sure,

42

Mr. Robinson is a great man, and he does think you're a jewel," she laughed and looked over at my father. "Now, are you telling them before she starts dreaming of Disney?"

"Yeah," my dad chuckled. "Ok, listen up akcrutes," a term of endearment he often used to grab our attention. "We are moving to a city called Albany." "Oh. Where is it?" I inquired, slightly disappointed. "Well, it's hardly two hours away from here," Daddy explained.

"Forever?"

"Yes," he replied pointedly as if no explanation was needed.

"What's there?" my brother asked?

My little sister danced around, still excited, not understanding the implications. My older sis, well, she was disciplined not to question and only do! She was ready for whatever our parents said we would do.

"But I don't want to move, Daddy. My friends are here," I whined.

"Dear," he said. "In life, we have to make choices that are for the benefit of the family. If you look around this place, there is hardly enough of us for you to experience your culture."   "Enough of us? I questioned. Here we go again, I thought to myself. My young mind was trying to understand what he had meant. I have always been an inquisitive child, forever questioning people, places, and things. Even at that time, I couldn't decipher why we had to see more of us to understand me. And in order to understand me, I have to leave everything behind? What was the point of introducing myself to a new culture in the first place? *"That was just the evolution of boundaries and self,"* the soul broke into my consciousness. "That's not fair, Daddy," I said cautiously, understanding the boundary of being disrespectful. "I don't want to go! You didn't even think of us!" I just crossed the line of being disrespectful. "Stop your foolishness!" My father stood up, evidently annoyed. "You think this town is the only place that has people? You will make new friends there. Don't allow your fear of change to be a reason to stay the same. Those who fear never branch out beyond stems. Come on now, get yourself together. Dry those tears."

My siblings didn't dare say another word. They watched as if waiting to see what my punishment might be. "Okay, Daddy," I retreated. I had no other option but to agree to disagree; after all, my father was the authoritative figure at home.

"We are leaving once you all finish the school year. So, no need to cry from now until the end of the school year."

My mom immediately covered for the relatively abrupt and insensitive manner in which my father had conveyed the news.

"Or most probably in mid-August," Mom interrupted as she motioned for me to sit next to her, to save me from myself. So, I did.

"You kids will have plenty of time to spend with your friends. Your friends can come and visit any time," she continued. I looked over at my mother, surprised at the last statement. Our friends could not visit anytime. That statement was to pacify me! "Okay, sweetie? she said as she wiped my tears and pulled my cheeks to cheer me up.   "Okay, Mommy."

"You kids, time to give your mom a break. Go outside in the backyard and play." This was a hint for the younger lot to vacate the area since the adult conversation was about to take place. We left as Mom and Dad had another private conversation, most likely about the move. My father always spoke to us in parables. He was helping us develop a thought-process that prevented us from getting caught up in our emotions. He hoped we would have a deeper understanding by not allowing our emotions to outweigh our decisions. I perfected what he instilled in me – self-defense – and now I was being uprooted in the midst of a new life lesson

47

– emotional control. *"To control one's emotions doesn't mean not processing them,"* the soul interjected. "Donald? I think we should plan a farewell party, especially for the kid's friends. This way, it might help bring a better mood about the move. It will be good for them as well as both of us," Mom said.

"You're right," Daddy agreed.

"Perfect then. I'll put together a list, and we'll get this done by the first of August. I will reach out to some of their parents and invite them as well," mom said as she stood up and picked the laundry basket. "I'm going to put these clothes away and check on them."

Chapter 3 – A Culprit in Disguise

The same day, my dad was sitting in the living room and reading his newspaper. The doorbell rang. He got up and headed straight for the door.

"Who is it?" he called out.

"Hey! It's your friend, Clyde," Mr. Robinson said cheerfully from behind the door.

My dad opened the door.

"Hey Clyde, you bugger," my father greeted amidst chuckles. He gave him a friendly hug and said, "How are you doing?"

Clyde Robinson had an unassuming presence; he was both polite and a very friendly Caucasian man. I imagine my dad appreciated his demeanor, perhaps because Mr. Robinson saw him as an equal and not as a Roots character.

Mr. Robinson hugged him back. "I'm good, Don," he said, wearing the same innocent smile. "Just dropped my kids to dance class and left my wife with them. Don't think I would do much good there, so I thought I would drop in for a bit if that's okay?" Mr. Robinson was a dutiful dad.

"Why not," my father said warmly. "Come on, in. Got some news to tell you anyway." Mr. Robinson came inside, and my father showed him the living room. "Let me grab us a drink."

Drinking was a common leisure activity among adults. I couldn't wait to grow up! Dad quickly fetched a bottle of rum from the corner cabinet and secured his place on the couch next to Mr. Robinson in the living room. Like clockwork, my mom heard the invitation and immediately brought out a plastic bowl of ice and a chaser. She exchanged a quick hello with a smile and disappeared into her kitchen space. We all knew our roles before we were asked.

The television, as usual, displayed a boxing match since it was my father's favorite sport. As he poured a drink for Mr. Robinson, he began to share what he had been longing to discuss.

"So, you know how I've been saying for some time about moving to a new place to give my family a better opportunity to experience their culture?" my father said matter-of-factly.

"Yeah, you've mentioned that," Mr. Robinson spoke as he nodded. "You've been saying that for three years now," he smirked.

"Hahaha… Yeah," my father mocked. "Well, timing is everything, my friend. I don't rush into decisions.

"Hm. I know," Mr. Robinson said.

"Well, the time is now."

"Okay," Mr. Robinson said, putting in extra emphasis on the word. "Where are you moving and when?" he asked pensively.

"Ah!" my dad sighed. "August and Albany," he changed his posture on the couch and continued. "I've given it quite a lot of thought, you know."

"I know," Mr. Robinson supported. "I mean, you've taken three good years to figure this out. You must have well-thought it out." My father nodded to which he added, "How does the family feel about it?"

"More or less, they understand as much as they can. It took some time to convince Sharon and the kids, well,…" more specifically speaking, my father confessed. "They'll have to be okay. It is for their benefit."

My brother and sisters were playing outside, and I curiously saw Mr. Robinson's car pull up, so I made my way back inside to go to the bathroom.

I opened the door, and my mom, says, "What are you doing inside?" Was this a trick question? Did I come into the wrong house?

Don't I live here? I quickly snapped back into reality and said, "I'm coming in to use the bathroom." I know this for the fact that I walked into the living room during the most pressing conversations because my dad and Mr. Robinson immediately stopped talking as I barged in.

"Mr. Robinson!" I jumped excitedly and hugged him longingly.

"Hey, pretty girl," Mr. Robinson mimicked my tone. I stepped back and put on my usual childish pout dramatically. If anyone could possibly influence my dad that moving was a bad idea, it was Mr. Robinson. He adored me. This was my time to make it count.

"Alright now," my dad reacted.

"What's wrong, Nikki?" Mr. Robinson asked.

"Mr. Robinson. Daddy is moving us far away. I mean, very far away. I won't be able to see my friends anymore," I whined. Mr. Robinson would always listen to me carefully and respond softly, which is why the stubborn child in me would come to life in his presence.

"Dear," Mr. Robinson said politely. "I'm sure your dad is doing what is best for the family."

My father smiled at him and glared at me. "Nikki. Stop complaining to Clyde; he's not going to change my mind. Don't try to play any fast moves here, you hear me?"

I wanted to say, *no, I do not hear you,* but that would have been like playing with my life, and I knew better. "He is not going to help you change my mind. Aren't you are supposed to be outside? G'wan back outside," he scolded.

"Okay, Daddy, but I have to use the bathroom first" I hunched down my shoulders and hanged down my head.

"Okay then," he said. "Mek'aste!"

"Okay," I said, slowing walking towards the bathroom, defeated.

"Bye, Nikki," Mr. Robinson needled. "Stay as sweet as you are." I could hear Mr. Robinson rummaging in his pocket, filled with coins. "Here. Wait! I've got something for you!" Bingo, my sulking paid off, although it did not get me what I wanted. I benefitted from my one-man show.

I perked up and ran back to Mr. Robinson. I was familiar with this gesture of his. He'd often give me chocolates or change for that matter. I greedily accepted as always and walked away.

"Nikki," Daddy said sharply. "Where are your manners?"

"Oh, thank you, Mr. Robinson," I self-corrected.

In my family, the rules were indisputable. Adults always had the final word. We were not supposed to question them and had to keep our manners in check. Another custom that was strictly practiced in our place was that no adult had first names. We were always to address them with Mr. Mrs. or Miss. Kids were to be seen, not heard. I knew I was being heard a bit too much right now. Just then, my eyes fell on my father, who was glaring at me. His stare was a complete conversation. I knew what to do.

"Outside," he strictly said, and I immediately did as was commanded – no bathroom break.

It was a hot summer day. Heat kissed our neighbor's sunburned faces. Perched on the branches, the birds sat silently looking for a sprinkler system, and the grass stood still and too hot to move. Movements by people were to create a deliberate wind or to quench their thirst. We were standing outside in the piercing heat of the sun, selling Jamaican style lemonade. It became a hot neighborhood commodity. My little sis drew in the customers with her cuteness. My older sis was supervising my brother and I to make sure we address the customer respectably. If not, she would be sure to report back to Mom and Dad to learn the basic customer dealing and discipline. Who knew we were being trained for the corporate world? It was a way for our mother to keep us busy until she needed us to do anything indoors. She was inside playing a mix of the 33 rpm records, from a range of Marty Robbins to Desmond Dekker, while preparing food for our farewell party tonight.

Mom was in the kitchen when the doorbell rang. She reached for the door with oven mitts still in her grip.

"Who is it?" she asked from the other end of the door.

59

"It's Clyde."

My mother pulled open the door. "You are early, Clyde!" she informed. "Donald is not home right now. He's out running some errands for me. Come on, in though" She widely opened the door and welcomed him. "Make yourself at home."

It is a Jamaican tradition to make everyone feel at home. I think Mr. Robinson enjoyed coming over because we made him feel like he was on vacation, experiencing our culture of food, drinks, and music.

"Okay," Mr. Robinson said. "It seems like it's going to be quite the party tonight! The music is good, and the food also smells great."

She allowed him in and closed the door behind him.

"What are you cooking?" He questioned.

"Don't you worry, when you come back later tonight, you will know soon enough. Listen, I've got a few more things to finish up in the kitchen," she said as she led him to the couch.

"Not a problem, I'm waiting for my wife and kids to finish up from dance class. How long will it take for Donald to be back?"

"Not too sure," Mom said. "Forty minutes, or so."

"Oh well," he stood up. "I should go home and come back," he paused, "– unless I can help you with something?"

"Oh no," Mom gave her head a disapproving shake. "Don't be silly. You are just like family. Relax," she said politely. "Stay."

Mr. Robinson made himself comfortable on the couch, and Mom headed to the kitchen.

"Oh, and by the way," as she recalled something and popped her head from the kitchen wall, "if you don't mind, could you get the door if anyone knocks?"

"Oh, sure I will," he said.

"And, make yourself a drink and turn up the music too if you want," Mom smiled. "Don't worry; the festivities can start even if you are a couple of hours early."

Mr. Robinson snickered. "You don't have to tell me twice." He got up, went to the bar, and poured himself a stiff drink. "And yes, I'll get the door. You go finish what you need to."

Here I come, darting in the house to see Mr. Robinson. Time to make some more money.

Before making my way to him, my mom tells me to go upstairs to clean my room, and not to make her repeat herself.

So, I ran past Mr. Robinson hurriedly to finish cleaning my room and get back downstairs.

"Hey, Mr. Robinson."

"Hello, pretty girl!" he said.

Mom popped her head in from the hallway for a brief conversation with Clyde. "The kids are excited to see their friends tonight. But they can't bring friends into the room with games and toys sprawled out in her room, Nikki knows

better," Mom says, justifying her authority."

Just then, her pressure cooker whistled.

"Lawd!" she yelped. "Let me go and finish up

this cooking." She went inside, speaking,

"Remember, you got to listen out for the door

for me!"

Mr. Robinson got up and turned up the

music. He poured himself a few more shots and

gulped it down in a swig.

Over the thump of loud music, I

remember hearing heavy footsteps stomping up

the stairs. A minute later, I spotted Mr. Robinson

at my bedroom door. I excitedly and happily

greeted him. I was glad it was not my mother

who came to monitor me as I straightened up my

room.

"I'm cleaning my room and getting ready before my friends come over," I replied.

"I heard, that's what your mom said!" he amusingly replied. "Hey, do you have some interesting games that we can play before your guests arrive?" He guzzled down his drink.

"Yes," I rejoiced. "I have lots of them. Let me see…" I turned to the closet. Before I could finish my sentence, Mr. Robinson said, "Make sure it's an interesting one."

"I will," I told him.

.   *This is your personal space. Never let anyone come near this space unless you know they have good intentions*; my dad's voice rang in my head. Dad taught me to defend myself against all personal space infringement. Here, I didn't know what to do. Mr. Robinson suddenly

65

covered my mouth and began kissing me all over the place. It was at that time I was introduced to a feeling I wasn't familiar with before. I didn't know how to respond. My voice was silenced.

"You should've reacted when you sensed the touch wrong," the soul counseled. *"He broke into your personal space."*

His fingers became a part of my body. Though I knew it was wrong, it felt wrong too, but I didn't know how to respond. Even if I sensed it, my body didn't know how to push this man back. I was reacting to a feeling I did not want to experience.

"But that was your personal space," the soul reinforced.

I was suffocating too! My mind was numb as he synchronically pressed himself against me. It was as if we were dancing while he kept kissing me from time to time, with his liquor breath. I didn't know what to do. More than that, I knew for a fact that he was my parents' friend, and I confused him for my friend as well. My parents said he was a good man, and I believed them. When this came from a good man, I doubted my instincts.

"You wounded me, Nikki. It wasn't just your body that suffered," the soul said sorrowfully.

I remained silent and let my body escape itself. I stopped feeling anything; my senses went numb. Quietly, I waited for my reality to set back in. Mr. Robinson briefed me on the implications of revealing our playtime with anyone and emphasized how I would be responsible for ruining lives and the party if I did. Message received. My new life lesson. Suppression. Adults have the last word. Kids are only to be seen and not heard.

I didn't say a word. I kept 'the secret' and allowed 'me' to remain in the small town and physically left Plattsburgh – to find more of us. But I lost me, and that was the beginning and end of everything.

"Your inner voice was silenced, and you tried to normalize," the soul empathized.

And the music continued:

"After a storm, there must be a calm

If you catch me in your farm,

You sound your alarm

Poor, me Israelites."

Chapter 4 – The Wounded Soul

Day after day
seeking my existence.
Trying to determine
what is real, and what isn't.
Searching for who I was
before I became so resistant.

Wanting to know me
before self becomes too
distant.
Are my thoughts my own?
Or what was instilled in
me?
Are my emotions genuine?
Or what I've developed
them to be?
Looking for answers
Where I left 'me' behind?
Only to find questions
Of my life - over time.
Aching to heal,

longing to know,
if there is a remedy
For the wounded soul?

Days dragged on, and it seemed like I was
moving on, although not in the way that I had
imagined. It felt like resignation more than
acceptance. Sometimes, by enduring painful
days and nights of suffering, you grow a thick
skin and become entirely numb towards other
things. Time flew by quite fast. I was
disconnected from my perception of self. I
hadn't yet discovered who I was, and I was
inattentive to the parts of me that needed
attention and perhaps unequipped to know-how.

I borrowed a brief sense of comfort that alcohol and smoking could lend me. It had been ten years since I moved to the new place, a place that was abundantly populated with more Jamaicans. Still, I couldn't tell if I had perfectly blended in or simply disappeared. I say that because even though I lived amongst my culture, I was different because I was not affixed to it. Despite my father's efforts to keep us culturally connected, my parents decided what we keep and what part we should dash away. One of them was the dialect. Speaking proper English was imperative here! Living in this new place made me more of a gypsy. I became reckless with time and took actions without thinking about their repercussions.

As I grew older, I began craving the love of others. I blame puberty for that! After what I had undergone down the years, I developed a never-ending void of self-confusion. Confused about what I wanted and needed, sometimes without knowing the difference between the two. Whenever I wasn't served love on a golden spoon, I learned to lick it off the knives. Going to middle school was challenging, but I found my way by excelling in sports and school. My excellence was a great distraction from my past; the appreciations – another form of love!

After I completed my mission in middle school, I graduated and was off to high school. Around that time, I mingled with a new group of friends as I and was being launched into a new environment. The friends I made were going to different high schools, and I would need to relearn what works for me. I get the sense that feeling secure was important to me, but it wasn't

72

a thought I could put into words. I felt displaced again.

As I begin my first day in high school, I felt siloed! You see, I was not allowed to wear jeans because, well, I'm not sure why, but I think it was tied to some religious belief. Women were not supposed to wear tight clothes. So, the girls in our family were dressed in slacks, dresses, and skirts to attend high school. I stood out!

My hair was stiff curled with the hot comb, and I had turquoise pants and a pink blouse. A great first impression as it relates to what my parents believed, but not a good look for the first day of high school. I wanted to fit in, but the kids made sure I knew I was different. I was teased about my hair, my clothes. So, as I became aware of my differences, I developed my new personality.

A strong front, approachable, yet hurting inside. This was my secure space. I continued to do well in sports and built a reputation of not taking any crap from people. The kids loved my dauntless nature! Soon, they became my friends. And I ensured their security and protected them in every possible way. But that was not done primarily to win their good opinion; the protective instinct in me would surface naturally. It was good to be around me at school, but they wouldn't invite me to their afterschool activities or parties. Not that I would have been able to attend. I would have had to be home when the streetlights came on anyway, but it would have been nice to get an invitation. It would have at least made me feel included.

I wanted very much to be able to make my own choices. I wanted freedom because I was trying to find me! My parents were strict. No sleepovers. No partying with strangers. Church every Sunday. Girl Guides. Pioneer girls. Piano lessons. Dance class. Sports. Homework.

And most importantly, cleaning up my room because they believed that our free time must be spent constructively. Looking back, I truly appreciate the depth of involvement I had in extra-curricular activities. It allowed me to adapt wonderfully to my adult life. I did not appreciate it at that time.

Back in those days, our weekends were spent with my parent's friends who had kids we could befriend. That was a great friend circle I had because my parents were with us. Needless to say, these kids found and introduced me to creative ways of doing the wrong things right under my parents' noses while I was around the "good crowd." At 16, I lost my virginity in the back seat of a car – in the "good" crowd.

I was not connected to the sexual activity, but to the power sex exhibited, in the sense of the loss of control in wanting to stop. Sex got me the attention and brought along the power I needed. I sought after it when I had the chance.

My urges for attention, care, and love got me into the wrong crowd and made me fall for a man older than me.

"To deal with one emotional strain, you embraced another," the soul said.

Through one of my parent's friends' kids, I met a guy who I was fascinated with. He was everything I was not, so I became who he was. He was a high school dropout (originally from Detroit), a playboy, streetwise, and four years older. His name was Brandon.

I was not allowed to date, so the restriction of not allowing me to be with this ideal man, made my blood boil. I left home to live with him. Now Brandon was in control because I needed him. It started with yelling, pushing, shoving, and ultimately resulted in forced confinement and fear enforcement. But after each incident, the apologies were so intense and seemed sincere. The apologies made me feel wanted. And that's just how I allowed another man in my personal space.

I bent more rules and boundaries that I never set in place for myself. I wasn't prepared for many things, and I didn't take time to understand them either. I did what I felt was right at that moment. Before I knew it, I was pregnant. And then, the baby came. I self-distanced myself from the family because I did want them to see my real pain. I hid my pregnancy from my parents for about four months. When the secret came out, my younger sister got grounded. I guess they figured if they kept her under lock and key, it would prevent her from entering the world of curiosity as I did.

My parents were old school and immediately decided I had to get married because there would be no bastard children in the family. Just like that, the date was set, and the decision was made for Brandon and me – no other option. Right then, another problem gripped my family – it was difficult to find a church that would marry a sinner – a pregnant teen. Eventually, we found a Presbyterian church that said yes. I was married in the 7th month of my pregnancy and gave birth to a beautiful baby girl named Amber. I did not complete my high school education and had to drop out in Grade 12 to become a wife and mother.

One day, I was in my messy living room with my baby. My husband was unusually strict about cleanliness and made sure I took care of the house while he was away. My life became a culmination of all the chaotic moments that had led me to that point.

Sitting on the couch, I was puffing cigarettes and reading magazines. The center table was usually decorated with the typical items, a pack of cigarettes, an ashtray, a bottle of alcohol, my glass half-filled, and a baby bottle lying on it. Every few minutes, my baby would let out a cry, and I would nudge her bassinet to quiet her. The next minute, the doorbell rang.

"Who's there?" I called out, heading for the door. A loud wail followed, and I knew Amber was up again. "God." I went over to her, put the bottle in her mouth, and rushed to the door. I was tipsy and irritable at the time. The knocks continued until I could hear the person from the other end of the door.

"Hey," said a voice from behind the door. "It's your sidekick."

I put the cigarette down in the ashtray, and headed for the door, and opened it.

"Darn! I forgot you were coming over," I said, come on in." I made room for her to get in and closed the door behind her. A baby's squeal echoed in the hallway. I hurried to the living room and saw Amber whining in the bassinet.

"Jodi! You woke her up again." I picked the baby and began rocking her. "Do you even know the amount of time and effort it takes to send this little one to sleep? She keeps waking up time and again. Swear, taking care of her is not an easy job!"

"I understand," Jodi sighed, stroking Amber on the back. "But you are doing it so well, and you look good too. Doesn't look like you gave birth to her only three months ago." She made herself comfortable at home, walking around the center table and picking up the TV remote.

"Thanks," I said. "But, I do nothing to maintain that."

"You'll be a great mother. God knows, I never imagined you playing this role that well."

"I'm not sure about that," I said matter-of-factly, placing Amber back in the bassinet. I was not sure if it was a compliment since it was coming from Jodi. Besides, where was her point of reference? I met Jodi as an ex-girlfriend of one of Brandon's friends. She was a hustler, smart-mouthed, didn't care about anything, and I loved her carefree spirit! Plus, she did not abandon me after I had my kid, unlike my "scholarly" friends.

"I don't know if I'd be an ideal mother or something, but there's one thing I know for sure, and that is," as I glanced down at my baby, "I don't want her to grow up hearing or being pitied over my story."

"Honey," Jodi said plainly. "You don't have to, because your parents have money." I grabbed a glass and poured Jodi a drink.

My dad was able to open his automotive repair shop, which was quite successful. My mother was an RN. They lived comfortably, and I always had to listen to their sacrifice stories about pursuing their goals. They focused - I did not. I think that was the main message!

"I am her parent. They aren't!" I snapped.

"Easy, girl." Jodi raised her hand in defense. "That was a joke." She slumped back on the couch. "Besides, what do you plan on doing? Working?" she chuckled, then quickly stopped after seeing my reaction. "You might need some help from the government. Why aren't you working?"

"No chance!" I corrected her right away. "No welfare for me. I do want to work, but I haven't figured out how."

"Got it," Jodi said. She glanced around the room as if looking for something. "By the way, where's your husband?"

"He's at work," I said, looking down at my wristwatch as I sensed my first hit of nerves, "but might be home shortly. I should work to help with the bills. Don't you think?"

"Should?" she pointed. "You're still thinking about it?"

"Yeah," I sighed. "Brandon thinks this isn't the right time for me to work."

"You gotta be kidding me," Jodi grumbled. "So that he can monitor you?" She snorted. "He's so controlling."

"Okay, now," I put up an act of being pissed. "Don't get started!" I looked away so she couldn't read my eyes. "He just wants me to stay home with our daughter, plus we can't afford daycare at this time."

"Okay," Jodi said, clearly hiding her annoyance. "Then what about your parents? Why are you so against them watching her?"

"Because that's what they expect me to do!" I snapped. "Plus, I am not ready to hear all those lectures of what I did or didn't do with my life." I paused and tried sipping down the anger. "I only call them in times of major need. Hopefully, when the time comes, I'll be able to build up enough courage to work out some

babysitting arrangements with my parents."

"Courage?" She marveled. "To talk to

one's parents?" Jodi was a good friend and one

of the well-wishers, so I often let her scold me.

"You are on your own now, so who gives a shit

about what they think?" she added.

"You aren't getting it, Jodi," I said

grimly. "My parents are from the islands – old

thinking! It's a much different wheel!"

"Still… but let's be realistic," she took a

deep breath. "What kind of job do you think

you'll get? What about the…"

"Why do you ask so many questions?" I

interrupted. I had enough and was sick of her

questions. "Listen," I glanced down at my watch

and continued, "I will find something. You have to go now."

I was trying to hurry her out because I knew my husband would be home in no time. "I will call you later, okay?" I told her. "I have to clean the apartment before Brandon arrives."

"You act like I have to be out before he gets here,"

she said, clearly offended.

"You do!" I demanded. "Or else he will think that I haven't done anything all day."

"Whoa! Sounds like Romeo is a Rambo! She stood up and began to leave.

"C'mon," I said, showing her the door. "We'll chat later. Now Go!"

"Going," she droned.

I closed the door and checked on Amber. Sitting back at my place, I made myself a drink, downed it, and started folding clothes.

"There is always knocking before the good and the bad news," the soul contemplated.

"Yes," I said, and I knew who it was."

"You knew, yet you didn't know."

Chapter 5– The Check-In

"Light always finds a way; such is its nature. No matter how dark the night gets, it is bound to succumb to the morning—the dawn breaks. The sun is destined to rise and project its rays to expose what is hidden. The light leaves no corner unchecked. The earth is its medium in its entirely. No matter where you hide or how many doors you shut close on its face, it still finds you because it's meant to occupy the darkest corners," the soul explained.

"And so, it did.," I agreed with the soul. It knocked on my door!

Right as Jodi departed, I heard another knock on my door. I shot up and meandered down the hallway, thinking that Jodi must have forgotten something. But no. I flung open the door and saw a bright face I was acquainted with.

"Oh, hi, Eva," I mouthed in disappointment. "What brings you here?"

Eva was the ray of the sun and me, the resident of darkness. My eyes weren't used to her radiance, so I'd often flinched or squinted in her presence.

"Hey, how are you?" She leaned in and gave me a motherly hug, the display of a sweet gesture to greet me.

I only allowed her to hold it for a brief second and pulled back in an instant. "I'm good. Come on in." She followed me to my living room and secured a place on the couch. She looked over at Amber and gently patted on her cheek.

"You have a beautiful baby girl," she sweetly intoned. "What's her name?"

I thought to myself, what was she expecting? A devil-possessed child because I had left the church?

"Thank you," Her name is Amber. I plainly said, looking over at my daughter, who was peacefully asleep in the bassinet.

"So, how's it going? Motherhood and everything?" she asked cheerfully.

"Oh, you know." I shrugged. "I'm doing well. Life is life. My husband is working things out, and we are trying to keep things together, you know, baby and all."

"Oh," Eva gently put a hand on my shoulder out of concern. I turned and gave her a puzzling look. Eva continued. "I'm sorry to hear you are struggling, but – "

"Okay!" I intervened. "First thing, we are not struggling! Its life – no one has it perfect."

"Sorry," Eva muttered. "I didn't mean it like that. I'm just saying – "

"See. Eva," I sighed but sternly responded. "I'm not ready to hear lectures about my life right now. Brandon is who he is. He's our daughter's father, and we are going to try to make it work this time." Brandon and I had a tumultuous relationship after being married for three months; it was an extremely abusive relationship. I had black eyes, scratches, broken fingers, a broken nose. I have many battle scars. I've tried to leave him a few times. Most times, I stayed because it was easier to live pretending; we were doing better than to face embarrassment from the outside world. Brandon and I had public fights; he didn't care where we were; he would make a scene. At times, I would make a scene to be saved, but people just wanted to mind their own business. Eva was probably aware of our fights from the prayer groups at church. They share everything and then act like it was a nudge from God to check on you.

"Okay." Eva then nervously shifted the conversation. "Where is Brandon? How is he treating you?"

"He treats me like a queen. No one can make me feel as special as he does. When we argue, it gets hard for me, for us. But when we reconnect, it's like heaven." I chuckled. "You know what I mean, right?"

I constantly had to drive conversations to enlighten the Christians that I was doing well. My messages were scripted with happiness for Eva so she could take that back to the church. They would surely credit it to their prayers. I was sure this was a "check-in" visit.

"Yeah," She smiled. "I know what you mean. Do

take things in stride. I want you to know that I care about you."

"Yes, I know." I suddenly felt a spasm of regret for being this ungracious to her. "Do you want a drink?" I asked, in an attempt to compensate for my attitude. "I don't have anything non-alcoholic except water and formula." I chuckled.

"Oh, no. I'm not staying here long," she said. "I did want to mention that I saw your mom the other day." I couldn't control my eye rolls. Eva noticed it and still went on. "She told me that you might have some free time, so I was hoping if you could join us as a volunteer at the church once a month on Saturdays. We are always in need of an extra set of hands for our community events."

Confirmed! This was a church visit and a lure visit.

"I need an extra set of hands too since my daughter doesn't spare me enough time to scratch my head," I answered. "It will be tough for me to help out."

"You can bring Amber along if that will help," she insisted.

"Oh, come on, Eva." I stopped her right there. "My biggest concern right now is to earn bread and butter for my family. I can't waste my time and energy, doing things for free."

"Nicole," she stated softly. "Volunteering isn't a profession or some kind of job that you should consider doing or not doing for free. It's just that doing things for the disadvantaged increases one's gratitude and peace of mind. That's how you should think about it."

No is never an answer to a question for Christians. Keep pressing until the subject gives up!

"Well, I completely understand, but truth be told, I am disadvantaged right now. The only people providing for me are my man and my parents." I looked over at her as she was listening to me quite intently. "By the way, I'm almost too sure my mom set you up to do this. Tell me honestly now."

"No, that's not true," Eva defended. "She just expressed some concerns that you don't hang out with your old friends anymore."

"Eva. Things don't remain the same once you have a baby. Life has changed for me big time. No one wants to reach out to me with a kid and all, so I've closed the door to people who don't care anymore and started lining up what truly matters, i.e., my family.

"Don't you feel lonely?" Eva had a pitiful look in her eyes, something that always turned me off.

"Lonely? Hell no," I injected. "I've got my daughter, my booze and my man – I am good."

"I still wonder why you'd always put on an act that everything was fine," the soul inquired.

I hated being pitied, I told my soul.

"My dear friend Eva said warmly. "Don't forget that I've known you for years now. I can read between the lines," She found my hand and pressed it softly. "Your eyes are the window to your soul. I've always cherished looking into them and getting to know you better, but today," she paused. "Today, I can't see the brightness of your soul. The window is closed, and you've lost the brightness."

I stood up abruptly. "Well, that was judgmental."

That was the nicer version of what I wanted to say. I was always raised to respect Christians, and truth be told, I always felt if I was disrespectful to God's chosen people. He would come after me.

"You try having a kid and juggling multiple responsibilities. Then tell me if your soul would be bright every day. Now, please!"

She stood up. "Don't get me wrong, Nicole. I just want you to listen to those promptings in your spirit. Once you start walking in the spirit, you will not give in to the desires of the flesh."

I walked over near to the couch where Amber was asleep, to find my calm spirit. "I

99

don't get it. Walk in the spirit?" I squinted. What

are you referring to here? Halloween?" I tried

lighting up the air because whatever she was

saying was beginning to leave an impact on me.

"Just stick to your core. Allow your

intuition to influence your thought process and

decision," Eva explained. Just then, Amber

started crying in her bassinet.

Thank you, Amber! You knew mom

needed a break!

"Yet, Eva continued, your soul reflects

your being. Just don't do anything at the cost of

your soul. One can't live without his soul."

I picked up Amber and was rocking her

while I tried to process the conversation that had

just taken place. I was hoping Eva would get the

hint that I had to tend to my daughter. Since I

was eager about maintaining the light tone, I sarcastically said.

"Well, that was deep. But I know who I am."

Eva stood up, walked over to me, and took my hand. "God always influences our directions; it's just us who keep listening to the demands of our body and flesh. I only recommend you have your priorities right while you're at it. Protect your soul because, after all, none of us is here forever." She paused and looked down at the bottle of rum on the table. "Also, just a bit of friendly advice – be careful with the drinking because now you have a daughter too."

The last statement was quite off-putting, so I sighed and got started. "Okay, first thing, I'm young. Young people drink, so do I. Second of all, don't worry. I'm not going to become an alcoholic, but still, thanks." I got up and started herding Eva to the door, "Now I've to get this house in order before Brandon comes home."

"That's no problem," Eva said. "Call me anytime you want, okay. Though you seem to have forgotten that for four years we were friends, and I want to remind you that I'm here for you."

We were friends because we saw each other every Tuesday, Wednesday, and Sunday church functions. I am so glad I'm not there right now!!

"Okay, girl. Thanks!"

"Would you mind if I say a prayer for you before leaving?" Eva offered.

"Sure, a little prayer doesn't hurt," I carelessly said.

Just then, Eva bowed her head, and I shook my head in disappointment.

"Father – God, we stand here confident in who you are and what you have done. Your creation speaks to your greatness. I speak to you on behalf of my friend and ask you to provide her strength. Give her guidance so that she may make the right decisions with her life as per your will. I plead you that whatever it takes, draw her closer to you and protect her life in the process, in your Mighty Name. Amen," Eva proclaimed.

"Thanks," I tried shooting a genuine smile. "Hope to see you again soon."

"Do call me whenever you can, please? Okay? I'll also call from time to time to check on you," Eva stated.

"Bye, friend," I said and almost shoved her outside. "As if prayer changes anything," I shrugged after closing the door behind her. "It doesn't change me."

I received some really good advice, but I had no time for perfect people, especially when my life was less than perfect.

Chapter 6 – The Beast

Another pounding on the door. Nicole had people coming over to her place that day. From Jodi, Eva to this furiously urgent knocking. The door banging continued, more desperately this time. I was puffing on cigarettes and had a glass of rum on the table. Amber was asleep in the bassinet, and I was lost in thoughts when I heard the irritating knock. Who was disturbing my vibe now? I shot up, butt out my cigarette in the ashtray, and headed hurriedly for the door.

"Who is it?" I asked, having no idea of who it could be.

"Hey, sweets, open the door," said a familiar voice.

I flung open the door and found him standing on the doormat.

"Hey… love. How are you?" I mouthed between heavy breaths. As I was speaking, I could hear my heart thudding in my chest. It was the result of both fear and the quick sprint to the door.

"I'm goo-" he trailed off. His broad smile flipped into a frown soon as his gaze fell on something. "Why did you put the bolt on the door?" he challenged.

"Umm…" I hesitated for a bit, wondering where the hell was his key, and then attempted to respond in a kinder manner.

"I locked the door like I normally do, Brandon," I defended. "Because you usually -"

He pushed past me, his shoulder hitting and almost jerking my arm as he entered the hallway and glanced around. Brandon was exhibiting

106

anger in his body and tone. During my life with Brandon, I became certified in reading body language.

"Didn't you get the chance to clean the house?" Brandon inspected. I suspected that tone as an alarm before the fire, a siren before the storm.

Trying to stay calm, and not to exhibit fear since that would give him power over me, I confidently voiced, "No. Actually, I had an unexpected company today and…"

"Who was it?" he interrupted rashly. He was already aggravated; I knew I would be roasted by the heat of his anger soon.

"Jodi and an old school friend, Eva," I informed. "Jodi dropped by to chat, and Eva wanted to invite me to a community event that her church is having." He had his eyes affixed on me, not blinking for even a second as I spoke. He was listening very intently – perhaps to look for any excuse to get started on me.

"And what did you tell Eva?" as sweat began to appear on his forehead.

"I told her that my family is my priority, and I can't make time for that," I replied, hoping this caring statement would melt his heart a bit since his tone seemed to be brewing threats that could spill over any second.

"That was a good answer," relaxing his posture and relaxing his eyes so that they were back to their standard size.

I sighed, thinking that my last statement had saved the day. Slowly, the effect of alcohol started creeping in my veins, and just like that, fear was being replaced by annoyance.

"How is it that you have lots of friends coming over to our place when I'm at work?" Brandon was gifted at picking something out of nothing. "Why don't they come when I'm home?"

"It isn't like that, and it doesn't happen all the time," I enlightened him as my irritation began to settle in – probably because I had been answering similar sets of questions and addressing his suspicions every day. Part of the reason I drank and got high was my messy life; the other half was to escape the stresses posed by this man who thought I owed him my life because he was providing for our child and me.

"Tell them to call before showing up. I don't like pop-ins," Brandon commanded.

There were times when I felt as if I had had enough and struck back regardless of the consequences. One such moment stared me in the face.

"But they are popping-in on me, not you! So, relax," I grumbled.

Brandon sat on the couch, calmly this time, and puffed on the joint he had just rolled.

"Watch your tone and mind your language. I run things around here." He craned his neck to look over at the bar. "By the way, is there anything to drink? I see you have already started."

"I just started, and there's some rum, I think." I always drank before he came home to take the edge off.

"Okay, get it for me," Brandon ordered. He always had the tone of a commander, telling me to do things as if I were his servant.

"Why are you always speaking to me like that?"

"Because you piss me off," He spat back in an outright brutal tone. "Listen, I work long days in the bakery. When I get home, I'm tired, and I need you to know how to act. I especially don't want to hear any lip from you; I feed your unemployed ass! You got that! So, act, right!"

I am supposed to act right, I thought silently! I was pissed and casually ignored what he had said. I was used to this.

111

"Your baby girl is asleep. I am going to wake her up so she can see her daddy," I stated in the attempt to be the loving partner of his dreams – though I knew that his complaints were a perpetual loop. He would complain even if I lay down for him to walk all over me - he would say I wasn't low enough.

"Don't bother bringing her here. I told you I'm tired. Keep her there," he snapped. "Actually, both of you stay the hell back there and give me some space."

He sat on the couch, removed his wallet, placed it on the table, and continued drinking and puffing to his satisfaction. Soon, he dozed off. I was there in the bedroom, complying with his wishes like a puppet. Amber was now up and restless, so I bathed her to calm her and to put

112

her to sleep. I went to sleep shortly after.

Sleeping was my escape to peace.

Before the morning could naturally wake me from my sleep, I hear Brandon, yelling.

"Nicole! Nicole!" he screamed, and as he was sitting upright on the couch.

"What's wrong?" I asked, wondering what could have happened now.

"You let me sleep on the couch – are you looking for a roommate?" he screamed.

"I didn't want to disturb you," I stated matter-of-factly. "You told me you were tired and didn't want any noise around you, so I gave you the space you asked for."

"Disturb me?" he pointed. "How much f --king noise can anyone make when they are sleeping? I wish he would smoke another joint and relax. He continues, "Do you think I'm here to keep you and the couch company?" His pitch was rising.

I was too pissed by the constant bickering, yet I tried to answer his pointless questions as peacefully as possible.

"As I told you, I didn't want to disturb you. So, I don't know what you're getting upset about."

His expressions flipped again from downright anger to outright sweetness. This man was a hopeless bipolar case.

"Come here," he sweetly said.

I couldn't believe him. For a few seconds, I watched him closely, studied his demeanor, and then moved closer to him, wondering if the intention was pure. Contrary to my judgment, he grabbed me by the hair and mouthed in my ear.

"Don't you give me lip ever again!"

I pushed him off me since I had had more than enough. The element of fear did not completely restrict all my other available emotions.

"Look," I said as I shoved him away. "You've been talking and treating me like a piece of shit. I didn't sign up for this. If you want to keep doing the same to me, you should leave."

"I should leave?" he laughed wickedly. "Are you kidding me?" his voice became furious again. "You need me," he pressed. "You think you can be the man in this relationship or kick me out for that matter?" he asked in an insanely childish tone. "No f--king way!"

He punched me, which immediately drove me to the floor, then straddled over me and began kicking and berating me with each swing and kick. Trying to shield the blows, I was in a fetal position with my one arm across my face and the other across my stomach for protection.

"Listen, bitch!" he spat out with a kick. "So, you think you can fight me?" he kicked again. "Huh?" Another kick. "That's a sad mistake!" and yet another jab. No one was fighting him, so his commentary was to justify his behavior.

I couldn't ward him off. His beating continued to his gratification, and then stopped just as abruptly. When I was sure he was done, I moved from the floor to the couch and collapsed face-down. I couldn't control my tears. I felt like that there was a thorn in my throat because no more audible sound came out.

"Get up!" he commanded as he punched me on my back. "I'm all you got!" He leaned in; his mouth came close to my ear. "Listen, or I'll wipe your face on this floor if you don't get up and make me coffee right now. Get up!" he yelled in my ear. I jerked up, trying to muster the energy and courage to move. I wasn't sure if he was just looking for a better shot! I sobbed and sheepishly headed for the kitchen area to escape the assault and bad-mouthing.

"Bring me a shirt too," he snapped. "Stupid bitch!" He got up and headed for the living room. "Can't believe you made me start my day like this," he quietly grunted. "Nicole!" he called out again. "Where's the coffee?"

Wiping my tears, I hurriedly made the coffee, grabbed a shirt making my way back to the living room, and handed Brandon his order - the coffee and his shirt.

Brandon put the wallet on the table, took off his sweaty shirt, and tossed it on my face. He put the new one on and got up.

"I'm going to work now, so you know the rules," his tone, strict and commanding. "Don't be on the phone all day. I need the house clean when I come home. You got that?" There was no sign of regret in his tone and demeanor for

118

the way he beat me up. Instead, my tears made him feel more powerful, something I hated about myself the most.

"Answer me!" he ordered.

I couldn't answer him right because I was still hurting and sobbing, but I knew I had to.

"Yes," I whispered, hence, made him even more powerful. That same moment, Amber's loud wails hit my ears. Irritated, Brandon headed for the door and left. I knew that Amber was hungry, so I grabbed the empty feeder bottle from the table and made my way to the kitchen. I opened the cabinet, then the fridge, and cursed myself.

"Damn!" I was frustrated by then. "I forgot to get more milk and formula." I rushed from the kitchen to my bedroom and hauled

Amber, rocking her on my shoulder to stop the crying.

"Shhh… shhh. It's okay." I consoled my baby girl and worried about what to do.

Don't let anyone get into your personal space. The words rang in my ear and I realized at that moment I had failed myself again. First, it was Mr. Robinson, and now Brandon," I informed the soul.

"Failure isn't defined how others treat you. It is more about what you allow. You were only one decision away from changing your life for the better; you chose toxicity and stayed rooted in destructive behavior," the soul explained.

I saw the phone on the table and picked it up in an instant. I made a phone call to my mother.

Chapter 7 – The Assault

My mother received the call.

"Hello, Mother. How are you?" I asked.

"I'm good, dear. What about you? Are you okay?" she sounded concerned on the other end of the phone.

"Yeah, I'm good. I'm okay. Just tired," I stopped the buffer and got straight to my purpose of calling. "Mother, I noticed that I have no milk for Amber, and Brandon has already left for work. Could you please bring some milk for Amber?"

"Okay, I was just heading out to the doctor's office this morning, so I can grab the milk I have here and drop it off to you. I'll be over in about 5 minutes," she said.

"Perfect!" "See you soon. Thank you, Mother." I hung up and rocked Amber across the hallway, back and forth crooning 'You are my sunshine' only to stop in front of a mirror. The girl staring back at me was a stranger, tousled and weary. The past few months had taken a heavy toll on me, but I didn't appreciate seeing proof in the mirror.

A soft knock and I snapped out of my dark reflective thoughts and answered the door.

"Hi, Mother."

Faithful and fast! My parents would do anything for their first grandchild, and for that I was grateful!

Mom entered my home place and handed me the milk. She didn't even notice me. She beelined straight to Amber. "Look, I'm not staying. I have my doctor's appointment this morning. I just want to see how my grandbaby is doing."

She walked over to the baby bassinette and picked up Amber. "Aww... baby," showering her with kisses. She was busy playing with the baby when Brandon barged in. He saw Mom and shot a troubling glare at me.

"Oh, I left my wallet on the table," he played innocent in front of Mom. "Good morning, Mom. You're here early. Is everything okay?" as he hugged my mom.

"Oh, everything is fine," Mom casually reported. I brought over some milk for the baby. Nicole called me this morning to and asked me to bring it over."

Brandon darted an angry look at me, and I looked past his glare. I knew what I was going to listen to any minute now. There was another storm brewing inside of him.

"I'm not staying, though. I have an appointment this morning," Mom explained. Brandon was playing nice on the surface. Little did she know how he'd been treating her daughter. I hid it so I would not hear any lectures about my choices.

"Thank you, Mrs. C. You are too kind," he shot a fake grin in her direction, the one only I was aware of.

"Oh, not a problem," Mom said with a swish of her hand. "Anything for my little princess." The very next second, she urgently looked at her watch. "Oh, Lawd, the time! I have to dash out now," she hurried to the door. "Take care, kids. Talk to you later."

"Bye, mom," Brandon exhibited false enthusiasm.

I walked across the living room and closed the door behind her. "Bye, Mother, and thanks!" I came back to the living room to check on Amber.

"What do you think you're doing?" Brandon grumbled.

"What now?" I questioned. "What do you mean?

"You called your mother to tell her how I couldn't provide milk for my child?" It was the same berating tone, always.

"You're getting it all wrong!" I defended.
"That isn't even what happened. Amber was
hungry and crying. I noticed we ran out of milk,
so I called my mom. I only wanted to make sure
that our child had food."

"Are you stupid or something?" he frowned
as his angry mode returned. "Don't you have
any brains at all? Now your family will think
that I can't provide for my child," he walked
back and forth. "You know what? You're a
piece of shit!" he gnashed. "I should let you
sleep on the street like the garbage you are."

"Keep talking to me like that, and I'll…" I
stopped abruptly. My patience had waned and
was highly irritated.

"Or what?" he posed the vexed question. "You'll leave me? And go where?" The maniac in him had come alive.

I was fed up. I couldn't think straight, so I went to my room and started packing Amber's clothes and then my clothes. I stomped out of the room, mouthing, "I don't need this," I trailed off.

What I saw next shook me to no end. Brandon had the smoldering look of revenge in his eyes as he stood next to Amber's bassinet. He picked up our baby girl, opened the sliding door leading to the balcony, and held Amber over the balcony railing.

"You leave and…" he spewed as he held Amber with one arm, "and this baby goes over this balcony! Try stepping out now!"

I had never seen him like this before. It was the first time that I'd seen him willing to harm our daughter. The beast in him was getting more evil day by day. I did not recognize him anymore, nor could I keep up with his tantrums. I broke into a cry, reached over to Brandon, dropped to my knees, and pleaded for him to put our baby down. Finding me powerless again, he took on his favorite task of accentuating my fear.

"No! No! Please! Put her down." I hadn't known fear like this before. I did not want to lose my daughter. She didn't choose this life. I did!

Amused by my helplessness, he moved Amber more over the railing to play with my anxiety levels.

"Please…" I cried. "I beg you! Let her go. I'll stay. I'll stay!"

After extending my panic, Brandon finally came inside and put Amber down in the bassinet. I let out a huge sigh of relief and positioned myself over the bassinet. Amber was bawling, and I was crying, knowing what was next. Brandon used my body as a punching bag and took all his frustration out on my disobedience. He then pushed me on the couch and started with the beating. I cried and wept and pleaded. How could a man not think twice about hitting a woman with so much force? Why did he hate me so much?

No mercy was shown, and I was bruised inside out. And I stayed in the relationship subjected to many more defeats. Brandon put down new parameters. He had a steel bar at the door; he used on my knuckles when I tried to remove the sliding lock on the front door to escape. His beating escalated to the use of bottles, knives, and any moveable object in his reach. He rigged the phone, a rotary with a screw, so I could only receive calls incoming calls with no ability to dial out. I was isolated from friends and family. I sought quiet retaliation. I spat in his food regularly when I served him and felt vindicated watching him shovel it down. My parents had a radar to know that something was wrong, and saw me in various stages of the abuse, trying to convince me to leave. But I didn't.

My physical wounds healed, but my soul…

"The wound remained open with each similar experience. Your heart accepted life's disappointments and deemed them the truth,

131

your mind repeated its beliefs, and in turn, the

soul endured.

I wept from the heart many times. And I realized my tears watered my soul to help extinguish the furnace of pain. It was strange how I was thankful to my tears for melting my stone heart – I could think and feel again. These salty drops were my reminders of who I became - a person indifferent to sufferings and sorrow. If anything, these tears were my source of awakening and a blessing.

After bearing another brutal beating from my husband, I went straight to the living room where my baby was awake in her bassinet. She was cooing when I sat next to her and spoke my heart out.

"Mommy made some bad choices, my love." Tears streamed down as I continued. "That doesn't mean you are a bad person." I caressed her cheek as she giggled. "Your parents are trying to work it out," I zoned out as I said, "We are figuring it out. Your mama is just not sure what to do at times."

After pouring myself out in front of my daughter, I reminisced about the calls I had previously made months ago to friends who have now abandoned me.

"Hey Susie, how are you? So, what's up? Oops sorry. Did I wake you? Oh, okay, I thought – What are you doing after school? Maybe I can stop by, haven't seen you in a while? Oh, okay.

Maybe Thursday, then? Yeah, call me, I'll be home. She hung up. Hello! Hello!?!"

"*I know,"* the soul sighed, *"you were desperate to distract your mind back then."*

"*Hey, Deb! It's me. Nicole. You off today? Yeah, I know, but... Yeah. I was thinking of swinging by because I will be in the area. What do you say? Oh, okay. What time are you heading to the mall? Oh, really? Okay. Another time, maybe. Give me a call... You forgot about me or what? (Fake laughs). Sure, we'll chat soon."*

"*You need help,"* the soul said. *"You were trying to reach out – but you did not stand in your truth. You were a great pretender, and no one knew you. You do not even know you. The abandonment of your friends was a constant*

134

reminder of your emptiness reflected in

loneliness."

My friends were tired of my choices, and Brandon and I were alone. I lay on the couch and wept to exhaustion.

I had two dialogues going on within me as I contemplated my situation. One was my own, and the other – a voice of reason.

"If I had never taken these decisions, I wouldn't have come this far in suffering," said the voice of intuition coupled with regret. *"If only I could just reverse my hurts, my choices, and decisions... If I could just undo life and start again?"*

"You distanced yourself from family and friends only to remain in your bad decisions," the voice of reason stated matter-of-factly. *"The*

135

same choices that were there to lend you

temporary pleasure, but you never understood.

Not just loved ones; you also distanced yourself

from sincere and honest opinions."

"I distanced myself and silenced all the

reasonable voices," I agreed. *"As the hunger of*

love and physical relations clouded over my

sense of virtue, I argued with everyone,

completely aware that they were right. I silenced

all voices of reason, including my own, and

stuffed their mouth with theories of my

satisfaction in that precise moment. I was

stubborn and rebellious, I admit! I take complete

responsibility for this."

"How about your daughter?" the voice of

reason inquired. *"Sometimes, your weakness*

resides in your strength. She was both – your

pain and your joy."

I turned to face my daughter and admitted the things I dared not confess to the voice of reason.

"You are my strength, my weakness, my answered prayer, and a blessing from God. My little source of regret reminding me of the wrongs I have done that I shouldn't have done; my little work of hope that there is light after dark and my only grand earning of life." Amber cooed. "But there resides a pain too, a regret in the knowing that I failed you. Maybe because I gave birth to you at a very early age, an age where I couldn't take care of myself, let alone know how to take care of you." I held her hand and gave my finger in her palm. She immediately gripped it in the embrace of her fingers, a warm reminder that I wasn't alone – I have my daughter.

I kept wiping my tears as I said, "I'm sorry. Mommy wasted her years in delusions, and she can't mother you. The truth is, I don't know how to, either." I glanced up, calling out for God's mercy. "Father, hold her in your arms as I wear my badge of shame. She is an innocent responsibility, a pure soul, and a sinless being. She deserves better. God, what you needed from me and what you still expect of me can never be. I have nothing left to give, no-good deed in my lap to meet eyes with you or the strength in my legs to walk to you. There is nothing in me to give nether to you or my little angel. I'm too sinful, God, and too tired to continue."

I always reached out to God when I was in need, but he was also disappointed with me and never seemed to answer!

There were a lot of police calls. I specifically recall a brutal incident where my father came over with his gun and my brother with his baseball bat when a neighbor had alerted them to the screaming in our apartment. By the time the police and my dad arrived, Brandon fled. The police found him hiding in the garbage chute. How appropriate!

It was the new laws on domestic violence that saved me. If the police had "witnessed" my physical abuse injuries, they could arrest the assailant. I could no longer withdraw charges. Brandon went to jail, and I went to the hospital. Amber was in my parent's custody.

I guess God heard me after all!

Chapter 8 – Opportunity Calling

Returning from the hospital, my parents chauffeured me home, and brought along with them, my blameless child. Arriving back in the blood-stained apartment reminded me of the horror I had faced. Luckily, my mom arranged for her sisters to come and demolish and disinfect the lingering sin. They also replaced my phone and passed on "words of wisdom, one of which I clearly remember: "Do *not ever let a man put his hands on you! If you can't get them while they are awake, get them while they are sleeping.*" I am so glad I received this advice after the fact. My family was fierce and always coming through despite the storms.

The golden sunrays spilled through my bedroom's window as a reminder that light breaks through the darkness and that there was a new beginning nudging me to start anew. I couldn't fight against the sun's power, so I stood up and willed my spirit to move.

By now, Amber was napping, so I took a quick bath and then checked back on with Amber, and I saw a life I was now fully responsible for. I grabbed the newspaper on the table and got started with my job hunt. I flipped through the paper and scanned the job section. I eventually found some of them and decided to call them up.

"Hello? Is this Kirkland Vacuums?"

"Hello. Good morning. Yes, it is," said a girl with a sweet voice on the phone.

"Good morning. Yeah, I saw your ad in the paper, and I'm interested in Call Agent's position, is the position still available?

"Yes, it is!" she stated.

May I please get more details."

"Oh yeah, sure, First, I'd like to know your name and your age.

"Sure. It Nicole Cambridge, and I'm 18."

"Okay, and do you have any experience in this area of specialization?" she inquired.

"Not specifically, but I have experience talking on the phone," I chime to inject humor.

"That's great! Are you able to come in to complete an application, and then we will interview at the same time?

"Yes, I can, thank you," I smiled because I was taking back some control of my life. I haven't felt like I added any value in years.

"By the way, could you tell me how much the rate is of pay here?"

"Ma'am, that depends on your expertise and the number of clients you attend. The hourly pay is \$3.55/hr.," she informed.

"Really?" I gasped. "May I come down this afternoon to fill out the application."

"Sure, Nicole. Anytime, what's your phone number just in case we need to get a hold of you."

"555-7496".

"Great, thank you, Nicole."

I hung up, flipped through pages, circled another ad, and picked the phone again to dial another number.

"Hello. This is McDonald's Wonderland Road; how can I help you?"

"Good morning! I just saw your job ad for the vacancy of the cashier. Is the position still open?"

"Yes, it is! Hold on. Let me get the General Manager!"

I patiently waited.

"Hello, this is Brian, how can I help you?"

"Hi Brian, my name is Nicole, and I'm calling about the cashier position."

"What's your experience as a cashier?" he asked to my disappointment.

"I do not have any real experience, but I am a fast learner and willing to do whatever it takes."

"Okay, could you please fax us a copy of your resume or drop in to complete an application?"

"I don't have a fax machine, what is your address?"

"It's 250 Wonderland," he guided.

"Okay, then I will stop by later today. Thank you so much."

Just then, Amber started whining. I filled her bottle with milk and put it in her mouth. But to no avail. She was crying inconsolably.

"Oh my... Don't do this now. Please, please stay quiet as I am on the phone."

I made another call to Mom.

"Hi, Mother, how are you?"

"I'm great, honey. You tell me? How is everything?" Mom politely said.

"Oh, I'm good. I need a favor."

"Go on, dear," she replied.

"Could you watch Amber for a little while today? I am going to fill out some applications. It would take a couple of hours," I informed.

"Okay... I'll watch her. So, when will you come to pick her up?"

"I will come back directly to pick her up. "

"Make sure you do that! "You better do that. You're a mother now. You should be responsible – "

"Wow, Mother." As if I just became a mother yesterday! I hung up.

Just then, my phone began to ring.

"Hello."

"Hello. Good morning, am I speaking to Nicole Cambridge?"

"Yes, this is her."

"You just called regarding the Call Agent position. I wanted to let you know that the first available time for an interview would be tomorrow. Are you able to come then instead of today?"

"Okay, sure I can - at what time tomorrow?"

"Around 1:00 p.m. Can I confirm your attendance for tomorrow?"

"Oh yeah, sure, I will be there!"

I hung up and called Mom again.

"Hello."

"Hey, dear. How are you?" a man's voice responded.

"Oh, hi, Daddy. How are you doing? Is Mother nearby! Mother?"

"I'm doing great. What about you, you feel better? She's in the kitchen, let me get her."

"Every day, I'm getting better."

"Hello," Mom was on the line now.

"Hi, Mother! I just got a call for an interview tomorrow morning. So, I was thinking instead of picking up Amber tonight, can you just keep her until tomorrow. The interview is tomorrow late morning, and I don't want to go back and forth."

"Okay, I'll keep her, but bring enough clothes for her.

"I know. I will pack enough clothes for her."

"Okay."

"Yes, okay. Thanks, and bye, Mother."

I was thrilled. That day had a very great start to it. I applied for jobs on the phone and got an interview call on the same day. Everything was going upward. I have some extra time, baby-free, I should celebrate, seeped into my mind, so, with no more thought, Jodi was the friend who crossed my mind. She was always looking for a reason to celebrate. Deep down inside, I knew what I was about to do was not the best decision, but I wanted to celebrate the little joys as they were getting rare in my life.

Brandon was still in jail, and it was the time I needed to move the needle forward in my life, get some courage, and try and make better choices.

I cared less about Brandon. I was beginning to get over this man. The only connection, and it was not even emotional, was our child. I was so dependent on him. I had to learn to depend on me.

I called Jodi and told her about the plan.

"Hey, Jodi, are you free?" My excitement was evident in my voice.

"Hey girl, what's up?" she cheerfully asked. "What are you high on today?"

"Ha-ha... I will tell you. Listen!" I quickly got to the point, "Come to celebrate with me."

"Okay... I'll do that. All okay?"

"Yeah, yeah. Everything is great. I'm celebrating my job interview tomorrow. I'm on the way to being independent! Nothing fancy. I just got an interview call today that I called about this morning, and I got the interview call a few minutes later.

"That's great news!" she exclaimed. "You know I support you with any steps you take to make your life better – that was prison you were living in.

I will drop by in a couple of hours. Just need to wrap up a few things here first," she said.

"Sure! No worries. Pack some things and just stay overnight."

"Sounds good. See you soon."

Less than a minute after hanging up the phone with Jodi, the phone rings.

"Hello?"

"You have a collect call from Exeter Corrections from Brandon Elliott, will you accept the call? I hesitated but felt empowered because I had a choice.

"A collect call? Sure, I'll take it."

"Hey, baby?" The voice sounded similar but was friendlier than usual.

"Hello, Brandon, I paused, is everything okay?

"I'm sorry about everything, do you still love me?

I was given another choice but did not answer the question. Instead, I responded, "Why are you calling me? You know there is a restraining order, and we are not supposed to have contact."

"I can't stay away from you; you have my child, and I love you! Look, I only have a couple of minutes."

I thought to myself, I knew there was a reason for this call.

"I have court tomorrow, and I need bail money," he petitioned.

"Oh, my God! Really? You want me to help you?"

"Yes!"

"How, I don't have that kind of money?

"Can't you get your parents to help me out? Just say you need the money for yourself?" he pleaded.

"I'm not doing that?" I stated matter-of-factly.

"Nicole!" he spat.

"No!"

"But I'm your man! I need bail money immediately." He was desperate, angry, and helpless, a blend of all negative expressions in his voice.

"I don't have that kind of money. Call your drug friend, John! I said sarcastically. I was in the driver seat.

"Nicole, PLEASE!" he got louder, and I hung up.

I held my head a little higher, and it felt good to say no to him, and he could not retaliate. I hope he rots there! Numerous musings went through my head as I busied myself throughout the apartment. Then there was a knock at the door. It was Jodi!

Before she could even sit down, I started.

"Jodi! You will never guess who just called…"

"Who?" she questioned.

"Brandon, from jail…"

"So," she asked.

"He was calling from the county jail!"

"He was asking me to help get him bail! Can you imagine, ME, help HIM?"

"Are you kidding me? I hope you said no.

"Of course, I did!"

"It's celebration time!" Jodi chimed

"I knew you would feel that way!" Then getting back to the call, "If he doesn't get bail, this will buy me some time to work and save some money and disappear out of his radar, my mom has Amber tonight, so I am free.

"So, what are we drinking then?" she exclaimed.

"Anything that flows!" I couldn't stop myself from grinning. And that night, we drank and danced, smoked, puffed, and snorted the night away. It was my moment. I fell for life all over again, irrespective of the fact that it always served me happiness in teaspoons. Nevertheless, I never let go of the little moments without celebration.

Chapter 9 – An Escape

The funny thing about celebrations is that they don't last forever, but you can sustain them by drinking and drugging. Erasing the memories of molestation, I graduated from Brandon's abuse to the continued abuse of self. I trapped myself into that prison, not a blame game, but more of a victim mentality. I do not believe I was looking for rescue, I was looking for validation of who I was, but I didn't even know who that was. So, it was spurts of happiness that got me excited about life. Like today! Today the universe strategized on my behalf and set me free from Brandon. I was finally free from evil.

I decided to stay home and have my friend, Jodi, over!

"Cheers to freedom!" I cheerfully said. She raised the glass and clinked it with mine. "Cheers to a new start! Also, finding someone new," she winked.

I chuckled it away. I could see how excited Jodi was. She never liked Brandon and always pushed me to leave him for good.

"So.... what's the plan?" she asked after taking a big swig. "Are you going to his first appearance? If you choose to go, you'll be leading him on. You should forget that piece of ...."

For someone not concerned about Brandon, she sure kept up with his schedule. I'm sure she was making sure I was thinking ahead.

"I'm not sure what I'll do. I haven't gone that far in thinking yet," I interrupted.

"Nikki, you need a solid plan. Get a man, a gun, or something. Get started," Jodi joked.

"Hey… Stop, please. Don't be a killjoy now. I'll think of something later, but for now, please crack open something so I can concentrate."

"This, my love," she pointed towards a bottle of rum, "…will make your concentration stronger. It will make you braver." She got started in a dramatic tone. "You'll probably call him after this and say, *listen up…I don't want you anymore.* Get off my ass and find someone else's ass. Better yet – kiss my ass!"

I remember us laughing so hard over this. But also thinking, Jodi thinks I'm a coward. Laughing helped mask my hurts and gloss, overexpressing how I felt. I was tired of thinking and talking about Brandon.

"I can't call him now, but I will. One day!"

Jodi poured the rum in my glass and receded when the glass was half empty.

"Just pour, girl! Pour!"

"Yes!" she roared. "Cheers! Here's to a new uninterrupted beginning, and getting my friend back from the trap of that cockr..."

"Cheers!" I interrupted. We took a swig together.

"So, tell me about your job interview – the one that's due tomorrow. And for what position?"

"Nothing much. Just that it's a telephone soliciting job where you call and harass people. You know the same way I'm harassed every day."

"What are they paying?" she directly asked.

"Much that I recall, she said it's about three dollars an hour, plus commission."

"Don't tell me!" she snapped. "Is that even a job?" She did her mental math and came back disappointed. "You'll hardly get $120 in a week, something that doesn't even begin to give you a fighting chance. That's downright slavery!"

I sensed the first punch in the gut. She was right!

"This is my first job ever without any experience. Would hardly get more elsewhere. Do you have a better idea? Because my options are very limited right now."

"Look, Nicole," she looked me in the eye. "I know a friend who works at Club Envy."

"Oh, please! I can't be a waitress!" This was all that my mind came up with.

"I'm not talking about waitressing!" She let out an exaggerated sigh and begin again. "I know how much you love to dance. Why not dance for money!"

"What do you mean by dance? Are you referring to stripping?"

"Exactly," she said. "I mean – look at you! You've got the body – the right shape and good looks too. You can easily take five to seven hundred a week. And that's not even full-time work."

"What! A week? You serious?"

"Yes! A week!"

"Whoa!" I couldn't think straight. I started imagining if I had the guts to do what was required in this kind of job. But instead of vocalizing my thoughts, I communicated something else. "What if my parents find out?"

"They won't. Don't worry," Jodi said. She seemed confident, and I couldn't be more curious.

"How are you so sure?"

"Okay, Nikki, I have a serious confession to make here," she paused and hesitated.

"Go on!" I was curious.

"I've been dancing at Club Envy for the past two months and made around three grand. That's for working only three days each week!" She finally admitted.

"What? Oh, my good God!" I zoned out for a bit and thought about my chances of making money. "You think I can do it?"

"Well, if you'd like," she looked contented now because she had somewhat won in convincing me, "I can take you to see my boss. He'll inspect you first to see if you would be a good fit." She paused and struggled to find the appropriate words to deliver the next phrase. "Key thing to do is to stay liquored up."

I poured myself another glass and drank to my satisfaction while Jodi showed me the right dance moves. Consequences were inconsequential to me. Money and freedom, that's what I was looking for. The next day, I went up to see Jodi's boss, who inspected my body and validated my body's future as promising as an exotic dancer. He believed I could be a good asset in their world. I perceived it as a sign of moving forward.

"You were receding. You scatter your path with thorns that whenever one issue resolved, you opened the door of another," the soul briefed.

I don't know what I was thinking. I was young and naïve, who had the responsibility of her child and, at the same time, the dream to afford everything and not rely on my parents. I was always thinking about the present, the pleasure of the moment, the short-term planner and doer. So, I took the job. Jodi and I partied and worked together. We'd get drunk to dance and danced to make a living.

"You shattered your spirit."

It seemed fun at the beginning until I started feeling empty inside.

"You never took time to process anything."

Weeks later, I reverted to my state of unhappiness. Though I was making good money, something was missing. Peace perhaps. Repetitive wounds exemplified hurt, emptiness, hopelessness; I didn't know where to go or how to heal. My soul grieved. It was numb, no matter how hard I try to feel something. My heart's imagination conflicted with my reality.

"You spent your life masking and pretending everything was okay with your false circle of friends."

Somedays, I felt like quitting, but the money outweighed my reasoning. There were times

168

when I could not get a babysitter, and I left my daughter sleeping in the apartment by herself while I went out to make a life for us. I justified my ill-reasoning. My parents found out about my stripping and late-night abandonments of Amber and took Amber away. Looking back, it was a good thing for both of us. It allowed Amber to have some normalcy, and it freed me, while at the same time bonding me to the lifestyle I thought would help change my future. But the more I made, the more I spent on drinking, drugging, and impressing people who I thought cared about me. My freedom became my bondage, and I knew I had to do something different. Maybe go back to my parent's home. I contemplated how, so I decided I would need to talk to them, and confess my sins, make them feel like they were right!   I knew I would have to convince them I had an epiphany about life.

"The soul was wounded, yet it didn't make any sound."

Mom came over to my place, and I sat at a good distance from her. My body continuously gave me the creeps. I was sitting on the farthest end of the couch and hugging my pillow to borrow the little comfort it could lend.

Mom came over to my place. I was sitting on the farthest end of the couch and hugging my pillow to borrow the little comfort it could lend.

"Mother, I asked you to come over so I could talk to you coming back home for a little while until I get back on my feet."

"Sorry dear! The decision to move was yours. Once you leave, that's it! We support you in good decisions, but you just can't move back with no plan."

"But Mother, I'm not a stranger. I'm your daughter!"

"I want you to be responsible," she said plaintively.

"I am responsible. I live on my own and try to do the best I can not to rely on anyone."

"Trying to do the best?" she nitpicked. Then my mother stands up and starts imitating my dance moves at the club. "We heard you've been stripping. Taking off your clothes for the nasty old men out there to make money! We're so proud of you."

I exhaled. I saw it coming. I put myself in the flame, so I should have expected to get burnt. I knew my mom was about to break out in one of her greatest soliloquies.

"Trying does not make a living – Doing does, Nicole!" Mom opined with pain evident in her eyes. "We allowed you to land on your feet by paying your rents for months, and what did you do? You acted like you were on an extended vacation and had men run in and up you and God know what else, jeopardizing a safe home environment for my grandbaby. You need to use your brains to plan for your future. Not running the streets, hoping things will fall into place!"

"Okay, Mother! Are you done for today?" I was upset because her words were not helping my depression.

"Where is Brandon by the way?" she continued. "Are you still running with him? Or is he not working anymore?"

"He's in jail," I told her guiltily.

"Lord, Jesus!" her eyes widened. "Why do you only surround yourself with people who cannot do anything for you?"

"Wow. I see I am still your stellar child!"

My mother grabbed both my arms with both her hands and gave them a jerky shake. "Give me something to be proud of!" Realizing she was losing her composure, she immediately released her hold on me.

"Mother! I'm your daughter!" I emphasized. "Everyone makes mistakes, so did I. I'm young! Why are you always criticizing me?" I didn't realize that I my voice escalated beyond my control in the heat of the moment. I knew at that moment, my chances to restart life at my parent's home just went out the window.

"Listen up, watch your tone!" she retorted. "I'm not going to stand by and be okay watching you destructive with your life. I'm not going to tolerate it! We didn't raise you that way. It seems like the devil lives in you!"

"Are you an angel, Mother?" Knowing my convincing episode failed, I went for it! Even the devil disguised himself as an angel of light."

That was a turn-off. She stood up and had her enough.

"Listen up, and listen up good, for the last time," she began—her face tense in anger. "I'm not one of your careless friends you talk to on the street. You called me to come over and then speak with me like you are off your head. What is wrong with you? Are you high, drunk, or what?" she slandered.

I receded and glanced down at my feet, regrettably. I had completely lost sense of what I was speaking and to whom. "None of the above." I let out and tried changing the subject. "How's my Ambi doing?"

"Good!" she snapped back.

"Okay. I'll stop by to get her shortly."

"No, you can't because…"

"What do you mean I can't?" I interrupted. "She's my daughter."

"I know that!" She taunted. "But you can't. Your father and I are visiting your aunt and uncle since they haven't seen Amber in a while."

"Unbelievable! Do I even have a say in the matter? Have you forgotten that my daughter?"

"We thought you'd be grateful! After all, we're doing you a favor by giving you some time to party and strip! I mean, take some downtime."

That was off-putting and threw me down the tunnel of defeat. "Looks like you guys have already made the decision." I could've been angry, but that emotion didn't come. I could've plainly said that I would pick my daughter anyway. But I didn't. I suppressed my emotions.

"Look," she sighed and headed for the door. "Your father must be waiting for me outside." After reaching the doorstep, she turned and said, "We will back late so you can come and pick her up tomorrow." My mother left before I reached the door.

"Okay, bye." My voice was barely audible to me as I turned the door close.

I wanted to go with them but had no words to tell them so. I was an embarrassment. I did not recognize me anymore. Then I began to weep uncontrollably! Mad that my pain was invisible to them, but my weaknesses were so evident. I resolved to mask my misery to prove to them I did not need them.

I remember I drank and drugged to my satisfaction and danced until I lost consciousness.

The next thing I remember, I woke up in the hospital and asking myself, why was I still here.

Chapter 10 – The Reawakening

"Your past was not yours to recall. Your life was not yours alone," the soul hummed in a low, hoarse voice.

"Why did I live?" I mouthed in disappointment as I opened my eyes in the hospital. The hospital room was as devoid of colors as I was of hope. Its' walls were bland and dull white. My back was stiff on the rusty frame of the bed, whose worryingly thin mattress only aggravated my back pain.

"It was not your time," the soul informed.

"Flirted with death and still came back. I guess death isn't willing to carry me either," I said to no one in particular. There was no one in

179

the room, just me and my solitude. A square window situated right above the television stand gave me a view of the sky, its color reminding me of my blues. The two chairs located on my right, frayed with wear and tear, only augmented my loneliness feeling.

"You wanted to escape, but it's not for you to decide when to leave!" the soul emphasized with authority.

My soul and I had never really gotten along. It always seemed to want to usurp my plans in life. My hopelessly disappointing actions were a stark contrast from its bright and spiritual theories. I only recognized this when it vented about my choices and seldom seemed to demonstrate love. What is love anyway? What is life?

I must have babbled some inaudible messages to my friends because one of them reacted and called 911 to my place. So, here, right now is an act of love. Here is my life. Giving me another chance to make things better.

Much that I recall, my soul had been at bay for so long that it had truly forgotten the feeling of the shore. It finally won. I was still. As the time transpired, blur recollections of my life reappeared along with the longing to feel whole again and breathe in the open atmosphere. It took two days.

My solitude back home was interrupted by an abrupt knock on the door. My thoughts were interrupted. Before I could approve of the visitor with a *come in*, Jodi stormed in. She sat on the sofa chair on my right and heaved in heavy breaths.

"You had me worried for a second," she panted. "Just a second, though. I knew you would pull through. You are too young to die! There is so much more partying to do." She stopped soon after realizing she'd just became a rhymer. "Shoot!" she laughed alone. "Did you hear the lyrics I just rapped? *You would pull through... so much partying to do...*" I only watched her straight-faced. Sensing that her words weren't impressing my mood, she continued. "So, are you heading back to the club tonight?"

I shuffled in and let out an exasperated sigh. The fact that I was already battling something inside of me, I weakly let out, "No.

Not tonight. I mean. Not for a while." I had to fight the energy to answer her questions.

She gave me a sideways glance, sighed, and continued. "Look, don't get all tight on me now."

I had little tolerance for her conversation. "Me? Come on." I knew I must be coming off too nonchalant and dull for her bright mood, so I forced a slight smile. "I just need to rest."

"You've been in the hospital for two days," she reminded me.

Something about this statement brought my blood to boil. "And?"

"And... I knew you would pull through," she said.

This was my moment of enlightenment.
At this particular point in time, I needed
someone to confide in, so I began pouring out on
her. "Jodi. I still can't forget the feeling I had
before passing out. I had no control over my
body. I felt like two separate people were living
inside of me."

To my surprise, Jodi laughed. I was
shocked, and immediately, a wave of regret
washed over me. I realized I might have opened
up to the wrong person here. Feeling the strong
urge to prove my point, I continued. "I'm
serious, Jodi! It's an experience I've never felt
before, even when I was high."

"Listen, girl," she grumbled and stood
up abruptly. I could see she was breathy and
knew she was too high to exhibit empathy in my
case. "I'm heading out to the club!" Jodi leaned

in and hugged my neck awkwardly. "Welcome back, Nikki! Call me later." She walked around the couch to leave the room but paused and turned around. "By the way, here's a treat for you to help take away the edge. On the coffee table, she placed a sandwich bag with two rolled joints. I didn't respond to her and only watched as she struggled to speak. "Snap out of it and start living again!" She turned and threw her bag over her arm and headed to the door.

"Thanks." I mustered to say as the door closed. I thought maybe I should treat myself to the treat. But I refrained, and knew something inside me was different; the urge for a fix was not there. Instead, I sat in my thoughts and delved deep into contemplation of my life over again. Returning to the same life meant doing the same things I was doing before. Then my thoughts shifted to Jodi. This was supposed to be my best friend, who couldn't bother to read what I was feeling, let alone understand what I was going through. I considered her my closest friend, but even she failed to lend me a shoulder.

"Your point of reference was from your experience."

I couldn't tell my family that I attempted to take my life. They would surely use this incident as evidence to try to keep my daughter away. I stayed away and made no one the wiser.

"You are a great pretender, always masking your pain. How can you expect them to know you and what you needed when you didn't know yourself? You were not willing to embrace your truth."

The door-knock again, somebody was banging it too violently. It couldn't be a friend or relative, preferably someone who felt the authority of even breaking the door if they wished. Raising my pitch to match the loud thudding on the door, I let out loudly, "WHO IS IT?"

"Hey. It's me!" a familiar and angry voice blared.

I jumped up on the couch to an upright, alarming position. "Brandon!" I mouthed within my breath. "What is it?" I called out.

"Nicole. I just need to see you. It's been some time, and I miss you." Brandon was playing nice; I knew this very well.

"Brandon, I can't let you in right now. Why are you here?"

The door banged so loudly I feared it would break loose from its joints and fall, laying the path open for this brut to walk in on me.

"Why?" he sounded angry.

"I'm not up for company right now. Brandon, leave!"

With that followed another ear-screeching blow on the door. "I've been in jail for months, and you don't want to see me?"

I was in no mood to entertain this man. A wave of exhaustion ran through me that evoked a closed-off spirit in me. "Brandon, please just leave!"

"You have another man in there? Huh?"
he suspected.

"Oh yeah, Jesus!" I sarcastically said.
"You want to meet him? Leave me alone now."

I was slowly growing a thick skin and
developing an indifferent tone towards him.
Brandon had probably never heard me speak like
that with him, which inflated his anger. "So, you
got jokes?" he said amid his escalating tone.

"I'm exhausted right now so, –"

Another slam on the door.

"Just because you are behind a door,
you think you can speak to me. However, you
feel? I've been in jail for months!" I could
hear the frustration in his voice but was not
inclined to inject kindness into the conversation.

"AND I WAS IN JAIL FOR YEARS WHEN I WAS WITH YOU!"

I was at the mercy of this man to provide for my daughter and me in the past. I gave him the authority to treat me like shit and even begged him to stay in my life. But here I was thanking God that my need for him was depleted, and I didn't want to be around him anymore whatever the outcome.

"What?" he punched the door.

"I'm calling the police," You know you have a restraining order," I reminded him. "You are not supposed to be here!"

"So, you want to get my ass locked up again?" he grunted aloud. "You are a piece of shit," he yelled. And then, as a person who seeks revenge, thinking it can bring him peace, he

190

said, "I am going to see Jodi." I sneered it off, thinking that Jodi would never entertain him.

"You have got to be kidding me!" I semi-laughed it off.

He banged on the door angrily. "Yeah, Jodi! Didn't she tell you?" He yelled through the door. "She came to see me four times in jail, and I've been messing with her too."

I was shocked to no end. Jodi couldn't do this to me. I was her best friend. She couldn't play around with my man when she kept bitching about him and urging me to leave him for my good. It wasn't like I was possessive about him; I knew I was good with my decision of parting with Brandon, and it wasn't going to change. However, I felt the backstab ever so strong hearing Jodi's name in the matter.

Perhaps Brandon could be making this up deliberately to steal the peace that I was left with.

A lump in my throat encouraged me to collapse and give away, but I was a master at holding back. Instead of drilling him to narrate the elegy of my friend's deception, I shouted, "I don't care. Go find her and leave me alone."

He pounded on the door again, louder this time. "Bitch! You wait! You better never be by yourself!"

"I want to be left alone!" I whispered to myself. Silence and peace were all I wanted. There was no more knocking.

How did I get here? From always wanting to be around people to yearning to be left alone. Perhaps, people were only a distraction, never allowing me to experience myself.

"Peace is found in stillness. Thoughts grow in stillness, and it's only then the truth can then be revealed."

Hardly fifteen minutes later, the door pounded again.

"GO AWAY!" I screamed.

"Nicole? It's Eva," a soft voice spoke from behind the door.

"Eva?" I sprang up and reached the door.

"Yeah. You okay?" she asked from the other end of the door.

"Are you by yourself?" I quizzed.

193

"Yes, I am!"

"Good!" I was relieved that Brandon was gone. I opened the door and gave Eva a warm hug. "Come in, please. Sorry for taking it long."

"How are you doing? I heard you were in the hospital and got discharged today." Bad news always travels fast, and the resource hard to determine. Eva had a worrisome look on her face and showed genuine concern, so I left my curiosity alone and embraced Eva's visit.

"Yeah... I'm just too tired."

"You should make sure that you're getting lots of rest." Eva warmly responded.

"No, I mean," I sighed. "I'm sick and tired of it all." Before I could elaborate on what

194

was going on inside of me, my phone rang.

"Hello?" I weakly said.

"Hey, it's me!" said a familiar voice.

"Brandon. What the --- what do you want?"

"Look, I was passing by Jodi's house and saw the police and ambulance there. The neighbors say Jodi is dead," he casually said.

"Brandon! I don't have time for your games." I was so done with his rubbish that I couldn't bring myself to take in whatever information he wanted to feed me. For one thing, I couldn't assume the news to be true because I just met with her that morning. It couldn't be true. I need to move and get out of here and start over because I too accessible here.

"No, I'm serious! Jodi is dead!" he pressed.

I went on the opposing mode, not willing to believe him. How could this be possible? "STOP JOKING!" I grunted. "I HATE IT WHEN –"

"Shut up and listen!" he yelled in his typical angry tone, the one I am used to him using when he demands me to listen.

"What?" I was listening and on my feet by then. Eva was giving me a concerned look.

"She's dead!" he mouthed and paused for a bit. "I just thought you should know."

I lost my voice. My legs froze on the ground, and the world seized around me. There was blackness before my eyes so I couldn't see;

196

numbness running down my body so I couldn't feel; my lungs forgot to lend me oxygen so I couldn't breathe, and my mind jammed so I couldn't speak. The only sense functional was my hearing. I could hear two sounds then – my heartbeat and his voice as he broke heart-wrenching news before me.

"They're saying it was an overdose. Drug overdose." These were his last words before the line went dead. Suddenly the phone felt too heavy for my fingers to grasp, so I weakly placed it back. The next moment, I sat down and wept. Later in the week, I found out that the "treat" Jodi left me as a *welcome home* gift was a joint, laced with Helldust and Opium, the same combination that killed her. It could have been me, but my life was spared, yet again!

"No one knows when their time will come.

By this time, Eva was on her feet. "I overheard the call, Nicole. I'm so sorry." She came near and gently rubbed my back to console me.

"I just can't believe it." The words hardly escaped my mouth amid sobs. "She was... she was just here this morning, and..."

"I understand," she let out a sigh. "No one knows their time."

"I mean, how is this possible. Jodi was my age."

"I know," Eva comforted. "It saddens me too, but death is no respecter of age. That's why we need to live in a manner that..."

My blood began to riot, and I felt the anger building up in me over the loss of my friend. I didn't want to hear a lecture about how good God is. "Why did God let this happen? Jodi was a good person," I ranted.

"God did not create evil," she explained in her soft voice. "He only allowed it to coexist with good. Tell me, how do you define good?"

"She was good to me, that is all I know." I couldn't concentrate on her words; I felt the loss stronger than anything. Perhaps, I wasn't in my senses. I was trying to process so many things.

"All things are interconnected. Remember, all things. Good cannot be the product of bad deeds. It is against the principle of goodness. Can there be power in weakness?

Integrity in deceit? Wisdom in ignorance?
Power in weakness? Honesty in thieves? Good
in evil?" I knew what she was trying to say here.
Eva was all about her faith. I grew up in a
Christian household but hadn't been close to
such beliefs.

"She wasn't perfect, Eva. I'm not
perfect either," I said defensively.

"No one is," she politely informed. "I
will never be perfect either, but perfection is not
a requirement to know God; it isn't even
attainable in the first place. Every single person
is imperfect."

I stood up, resisting Eva's words. "I
know where you are heading with this. I just
don't know – "

There was usually a stirring of resistance when I felt that a religious conversation was about to be shoved down my throat. However, this time was different. I was cautious yet receptive!

"Look, no one knows when their time is up," she emphasized with more urgency in her voice.

"I don't know if I'm ready for what you want me to be," I gingerly muttered, mostly to myself.

"Time is fleeting. What are you waiting for?" she insisted. I was waiting to smoke the joint that Jodi left me. The timing of Eva coming over could only have been orchestrated by God to infiltrate my heart and to distract me from smoking the treat Jodi left for me.

"Eyes have not seen, nor have ears heard, man has a vague understanding of God's work."

"Eva, I must confess something. I have done so much, I mean, chosen all the wrong paths and…"

Eva must have studied the desperation in my voice because she said, "It just takes a step to turn your life around for the better."

"I have done all the wrong things. I'm just tired of it all. Too tired to continue with anything."

"I understand you're tired, but does anyone ever get tired of doing good? Just think about it."

"You have an answer for everything."

"I am not focused on having the answers. I want to help you! What kind of friend would I be if I did not want the best for you? She paused, then advised, "Let me pray for you." Eva enveloped me in an embrace and began to pray. "I pray that you embrace the truth, and the questions planted in your soul allow your heart to say yes to our Lord." I was only watching her silently as she had her eyes closed while her lips mumbled the ideal words for my situation. "Lord, allow Nikki's wounded soul to harmonize with her heart. Free her spirit from the lies she has been told and what she has told herself all her life. She belongs to you, Lord, and you have spared her for a purpose. I believe your love and grace restores and mends." My eyes began tearing up like that of a neglected child who gets support or someone who speaks on his behalf for the first time.

"Lord. Please have your way in Nikki's life and direct her path towards a fulfilling purpose. Help her understand that she is not capable of doing life alone. She needs you. Help her know who you are – the Lord who stretches out the earth and forms the spirit of man. In Your Name, we pray, Amen."

With that, she gave me a final hug and departed through the front door, leaving me all the wiser and shrewder. She opened the cages of my thoughts that were once locked up by my indifference. I was receptive and open. God has a way of removing things from your life so you can see Him.

I was born whole and innocent. Or so I'd like to think. But circumstances in my early childhood shattered my innocence and punctuated every bad decision I made. Although I believed in God, I always wondered where was He during my struggles?

"He never left you; you left Him. Every time you felt the prompting in your soul, you knew you were not making the right decisions – you still went ahead. You heard the knocking. Always," the soul imparted.

"When your conscience was undecided, that was Him in your midst. You chose to avoid His voice. His prompting.

Nothing in all creation is hidden from His sight. You made decisions based on your desires, what felt good for you, not what was

right for you."

As I was stilled, I find my thoughts

drifting back to the spiritual droppings that were

prayed, taught, and encroached upon me. Once

you know about something, it is hard to unlearn.

Growing up, my childhood rituals

involved Tuesday family night bible studies at

home and Sundays, church! It was painful at

times, but I recall the verses. Each session

started with Proverbs 22:6 and prayer! I

remember Romans 3:23, John 3:16, and Romans

4:8, and the lessons associated with them. *We*

are all sinners, and yet God still loves us, and he

does not count our sins against us. Because we

had to memorize them at home and church, these

verses were etched in my mind. In the end, these

messages resonated in me, and I started to

206

believe it! I had many moments where I knew my life was not the way it was supposed to be. I understood the morals and values that were instilled in me, yet I reasoned away what was right, in hopes that I would find my own "right."

I wasn't sure what my next step was, but I yearned to know God more. I didn't rededicate my life to Christ because "we all fall short." Attending church became a routine for me, but this time, I wanted to go because I wanted to know God beyond my original understanding. I read the bible and prayed more. It gave me hope. I built relationships that helped build me. My relationship with God became my priority. The God I grew up with was angry at me, or so I thought. But the God I came to know loved me despite my past.

I didn't experience many stable relationships for the longest time. It's interesting when you get used to things going wrong; it becomes harder to see any good. My life reflected that. I drifted back and forth in the comfortable past and into an uncertain future that scared me. My mind conflicted with my heart and was flooded with thoughts I needed to work through. My mother had set up counseling sessions for me to help me determine the demons within. However, after one counseling session talking about my traumatic past, the pain exploded, and I didn't want to cope with everything all over again, so I buried it. My family banded behind me on my path to betterness, and because of their love, I can continue this journey before with me.

Today, looking back at my detours, I am amazed at what I have overcome. My life is truly an antithesis of what it should be.

Once I began to heal me, acknowledge my truths, accept accountability for where I failed me, it was a butterfly experience. There was a feeling of transformation, but to truly be feel free, I felt I had to shame my past by sharing my experiences.

I refuse to hide anymore! My past has become my springboard.

My future was gifted with a man of God, my husband Darrick, who has loved me through my brokenness, cheered me through my healing process, kissed my scars, and held my hand through it all, so I do not have to feel like I was on your own.

Through it all, I have remained grateful and understand that I am walking in my purpose! I understand that my detours have helped me to arrive at my authentic self. I appreciate every day given to me to be an instrument of good and to invest in others. I am grateful God spared me.

Author's Note

Although my story ends with what could be interpreted as a clean separation, that was not the case. As with most domestic violence issues, when you decide to leave, it can escalate emotions. It did, there were multiple altercations, run-ins with the law, threats, and more order of protections. We were only married four months – but it took Brandon's deportation and 2.5 years to get the divorce. I am free.

With the help and love of my family, I was able to turn my life around. Every day is an opportunity to continue to rise.

I want to encourage those who remain behind their mask to choose your steps towards restoration safely. You are worth so much more.

Sheryl Hatwood is the Owner & Founder of Endless Voice Productions, LLC, a company that delivers innovative and creative playwrights and inspiring events. The debut of her 2017 off-broadway play "The *Wounded Soul*" was the impetus that propelled her to create the Annual "*A Woman's Worth Awards*" and "*Women in Business*" events. In line with her mantra to have internal peace, she has launched her aromatherapy line "TRUCE," which debut in September 2020. Having been interviewed by various media outlets including "*AspireTV,*" "*RollingOut,*" "*Unapologetically US,*" "*Urban Magazine,*" "*Westchester Magazine*" and live TV appearances on *Arise Entertainment 30,* and *TVOne -Madame Noire,* Sheryl continues to share her truth with audiences across many National forums and platforms. The 2019 WEI Trailblazer Award was awarded to Sheryl as an accomplished leader in the community, and she has received a Proclamation from the Westchester County Governor for the exceptional example she has made with her unique personal achievements.

www.sherylhatwood.com